| | | |
|---|---|---|
| The Wolf | | |
| The Fifth Gospel | | |
| Mission Impossible | | |
| Drawing Near | .................................. | 9 |
| But If Not | .................................. | 11 |
| Her Majesty | .................................. | 13 |
| A Better Pharisee | .................................. | 16 |
| Bones | .................................. | 18 |
| New Beginnings | .................................. | 20 |
| Trains | .................................. | 22 |
| Limping | .................................. | 24 |
| University of the Cross | .................................. | 27 |
| Light vs. Darkness | .................................. | 30 |
| Upside Down | .................................. | 33 |
| Freedom | .................................. | 35 |
| Recalibrating | .................................. | 38 |
| In Search of Sasquatch | .................................. | 40 |
| Mountains | .................................. | 43 |
| Innkeepers | .................................. | 46 |
| Going in Circles | .................................. | 49 |
| Sleep | .................................. | 52 |
| Certain Doubt | .................................. | 54 |
| Scandalous | .................................. | 57 |
| Fences | .................................. | 60 |
| Good Luck | .................................. | 62 |
| Eulogies | .................................. | 65 |
| Waiting | .................................. | 68 |
| Carried | .................................. | 71 |

| | | |
|---|---|---|
| Why? | ............................. | 73 |
| One Word | ............................. | 75 |
| Words of Comfort | ............................. | 77 |
| Everydayness | ............................. | 79 |
| Happiness | ............................. | 81 |
| Easter | ............................. | 84 |
| Wait For It | ............................. | 87 |
| Longing for Home | ............................. | 89 |
| Farming | ............................. | 91 |
| Shhhh! | ............................. | 93 |
| Feet of Clay | ............................. | 96 |
| Tim | ............................. | 99 |
| Delight | ............................. | 102 |
| Small Fries | ............................. | 104 |
| A KonMari Heart | ............................. | 106 |
| Encouragement | ............................. | 108 |
| Time and Eternity | ............................. | 111 |
| Adored | ............................. | 114 |
| Lord of the Feast | ............................. | 117 |
| Givers and Takers | ............................. | 120 |
| A Person and a Place | ............................. | 123 |
| Appointments | ............................. | 126 |
| Riches | ............................. | 129 |
| Two Lions | ............................. | 131 |
| Goats | ............................. | 133 |
| The Silence of God | ............................. | 135 |
| Our Cheerleader | ............................. | 138 |
| Night Shift | ............................. | 140 |

# The Wolf

My life was changed by a 13 year old girl. Her name was Anne Frank.

I read her Diary when I was in high school, a riveting account of a Jewish girl hiding from the Nazi Gestapo in 1942.

She hid in a room behind a bookcase where her father Otto worked. Anne kept a diary of her experience until she was captured in August, 1944.

Sent to the horrific Auschwitz Concentration Camp, she died of malnutrition and typhus three months later.

Two weeks ago, I saw an exhibit about her life in Europe and was moved to tears about her life.

But it was the video I saw there of how the Nazi's treated God's Chosen People. The haunting images bore deeply into my soul.

The Jews were hunted down, herded into trains, and millions perished. I have been to Auschwitz; there are no words.

As I watched the subhuman treatment of the Jews, I was struck by two words the Bible talks a lot about: the wolf and the shepherd.

The Jews in World War ll were hunted down like sheep without a shepherd. Devoured by the Wolf, the predator of God's flock.

Adolph Hitler and the Nazis.

The name of Hitler's military headquarters? Wolfsschanze. The Wolf's lair.

Other strongholds named after Hitler: the Wolf's Gorge. Or the Werewolf. His friends called the Fuhrer the Wolf.

The meaning of the name Adolph? Right. The Wolf.

The greatest enemy of the Jewish People was named the Wolf. So it is with Christians.

But there is a difference. For 2,000 years Jews have wandered without a Shepherd. And they have been the hunted.

Not true for Christians. Our Messiah said, "I am the Good Shepherd. I will lay down My life for the sheep."

Unlike Anne Frank we have a better hiding place. The Shepherd's Hand.

Jesus said, "No one will snatch them out of my hand or the Father's hand. I and the Father are One." ***(John 10: 30- 31)***.

That's a good hiding place to write our own diary. It has a much, much better ending.

Actually, a perfect one.

# The Fifth Gospel

One of the reasons "The Chosen" TV series has been a runaway success is because it shows Jesus as fully human and relatable.

People go wild over real people.

It is impossible for me to believe Jesus didn't horse around with His men. From potty stops to a sweet treat from the local bakery.

Can you see Peter arm wrestling with the Son of God? I can. Call me sacrilegious. I just think a fully human being has a few satisfying belly laughs.

And especially with the knuckleheads our Lord chose. Do you honestly think "how long have I been with you?" didn't come with a roll of His divine eyes?

I think Jesus was playful. And yes, always with serious eyes fixed on Calvary. His sacrificial holiness makes our life even possible.

Yet I think the Creator of the Universe also knew the value of humor. He created it. Might as well use it.

Jesus took His mission seriously. But His love also lightened things up. Sort of laugh or go insane in His crazy world.

At the end of his life, my hero CS Lewis was very ill. It killed him to resign from Cambridge. He brought all his books (can you imagine) home to his small cottage.

He had a live-in male nurse he only tolerated.

One day, as the nurse napped, Lewis built a wall of books around him floor to ceiling. The sleeping man awoke to a literary prison.

To the end, his Narnia playfulness was fully expressed.

Our daughter Whitney thinks she has a problem. She laughs out loud about the most dire of circumstances.

I think it's a gift. When you adopt three kids and already have three, laughter through tears is a balm from heaven.

Don't you just love a God who knows that playfulness helps our recovery and resilience? It makes our fears mangeable.

I don't want a plastic Jesus. I want one with dirt under His fingernails and hair on His chest.

The Man. Our God. The World's Savior.

My Everything.

# Mission Impossible

People ask us at times, "How did you raise three great kids?"

It's a fair question (because Whitney, John and Mindy are great) and I give a true answer, "I have no idea."

If you ever ask me to lead a parenting seminar I would decline with something like "Over my dead body."

Raising great kids is a crapshoot. Guarantees are out.

Good parents in the Bible had bad kids. Bad parents had good kids. Go figure.

I have heard it said that marriage is a calculated risk. As in no clue when you say "I do."

I think exercising the perfect blend of love and discipline with children in our Age is more like "I can't." It's a battle.

Add to our three kids the blessed assortment of 12 grand kids and you've turned our blender up to about nine.

The other day, in a session with a "parenting expert" the question was asked "When do you discipline your children?"

There was a quick response, "When there are three D's. Disrespect, Disobedience, Deceit."

I actually think that's good advice. Good luck in pulling it off in the midst of a meltdown – by the parent or the kid.

Again, the Bible gives principles on parenting but no guarantees.

Here's the best I can offer as far as kids loving life and loving you. It also applies to grand kids.

Just enjoy them.

See them as a gift. Tell them they are great and the best company you'll ever have is theirs.

Kids know when they are adored. They also know when it's dutiful. Something about "have to and get to".

I believe that even if parents are right, you can right them right out the door.

Our God is a Father who always treats His children with love and forgiveness. He runs and kisses his prodigal son in Luke 15.

He doesn't need us. Miraculously, He just enjoys us.

End of my Parenting Seminar.

# Drawing Near

Have you ever thought what it means when Jesus is called a "friend of sinners"?

There's one phrase that sums it all up: The tax collectors and the sinners were all "drawing near to hear Him." *(Luke 15:1)*.

Drawing Near.

Two groups that are viewed with disdain by the religious crowd in **Matthew 11** couldn't stay away from him in **Luke 15**.

Here's what's amazing to me: Jesus AND the irreligious were at ease around each other.

While others sneered, the outcasts saw something different in Jesus Christ. He ate with them. Sought them out.

And most of all... gave them fresh hope.

ALL of us have unsavory battles going on within us: faithful or fickle, attractive or revolting, clean or unclean.

Even among our very best friends, we dare not divulge every hidden part. The difference is informing vs. entrusting.

What if we had a friend who had no ceiling on what he would put up with and still wanted to be with us?

We do.

**Revelation 3:20**: "I stand at the door and knock. Anyone who hears my voice and opens the door I will come in to him and eat with him and he with me." Jesus is knocking.

And who's living behind the doors? The "wretched, pitiful, poor, blind and naked." **(Revelation 3:17)**.

Pretty much sums up my life on the good days. Now lest we forget Jesus power, majesty and holiness, we will all fall down speechless, in awe one day. He's also the roaring Lion of Judah.

But here the Lamb of God is now inviting sinners to come have supper.

We all know He loves us. We have verses on it. The staggering truth is He even likes us. Wants us.

Invites us. Leans in to us.

Our job? Just open the door... warts, wicked hearts and all.

His astounding promise?

He will draw near.

# But If Not

Many stories in the Bible blow me away. I say to myself, "No way I could even think about doing that."

For example, Abraham and Isaac. Lift a knife to take our son John's life. No way.

But there is one story that apart from the Resurrection of Christ gets to me the most.

It involves three Hebrew teenagers. Shadrach, Meshach and Abednego. You know the story.

But three words you may have missed about the story in **Daniel 3: 17-18**. I did.

They make all the difference between uncommon bravery and staggering faith. Dare I say way way beyond my faith.

When my furnace gets too hot to stand, facing impossible odds... three words get me through.

But if not.

Three kids who refused to bow to the image of King Nebuchadnessar, who turned his literal furnace up as high as his rage.

The boys were equal in their stance: "Our God is able to deliver us from the burning fiery furnace...BUT IF NOT...we will not serve your gods or worship your image."

Two truths: He can deliver. Or choose not to. In either case, they would not waver.

Here's what's staggering to me: They had faith in a Person, not faith in an Outcome. I want that, but fail so often.

I think God answers my prayers when I get the result I want. God says "honor Me to do what's right, I'll handle the rest."

But if not.

What hellacious fire are you facing or fearing?

Life's furnaces are a certainty.

Esther faced it. Three teens faced it. You and I will face it. Charging after Jesus is risky.

He can deliver you. Or...He may not. Knowing He CAN gives me great comfort.

Is He our Maker, Redeemer, and Keeper when flames engulf us? He is. Right beside us. There were Four men walking in Neb's furnace.

We will either be taken to heaven or insulated on earth. One way or the other, He will deliver us from our fiery furnace.

With no scent of smoke. **(Daniel 3: 27)**.

# Her Majesty

Seventy years on the throne. Millions lining the streets of London today at her funeral.

The incomparable Queen Elizabeth II. A devout follower of Jesus.

She once said, "Billions of people follow Christ's teachings and find in Him the guiding light for their lives. I am one of them."

When she turned 90 a book was written about her by the Bible Society. In it was the only forward she ever penned.

The title: The Servant Queen and the King She Served.

It summed up her life perfectly. She has now placed her royal crown at the feet of her Sovereign King.

She was a Queen who served the King of Kings—Who loved her, forgave her, died for her, and rose again. *(John 3:16)*.

She walked with people... millions of them. Always giving attention to the person in front of her. Never in a hurry to move past them. President or pauper.

Her Majesty was a part of our lives. Her faithfulness for 7 decades was a constancy, a secure rock in a changing world. She is now with the Rock of Ages.

Through the Blitz of London, 15 Prime Ministers, WW II...she never changed.

On September 8th, she did. She had a wonderful relationship with Billy Graham, to the upturned noses of the Anglican establishment.

The Queen wanted Billy to come for lunch, teach her, discuss the Bible.

One day, the famed evangelist said he wanted to teach about the lame man's healing at the pool of Bethesda. *(John 5)*.

By Dr. Graham's own account, the Queen'e eyes sparkled with bubbling excitement. "That is my favorite story!"

A cripple healed after 38 years with no one to help him resonated with a Royal who had scores of servants. The lame needed Jesus healing, and so did she.

Towards the end, Queen Elizabeth moved slowly. Unsteady.

But not today.

She stands with sturdy legs... Before the King she adored.

Believers shall see her again.

The Queen of England was also my sister.

Thank you your Majesty for showing us Jesus. Well done.

Enter in... to the joy of your Master.

# A Better Pharisee

How could the worst TV show of all time be watched by millions for 27 years?

How could adults acting like dysfunctional babies be the hit of daytime TV?

Welcome to the Jerry Springer Show. Perhaps you remember it.

The question is: Why? What caused this display of human idiocy to be celebrated as "America's Guilty Pleasure?"

I think I know the reason. It made us feel better about ourselves.

At least, we reasoned, we're not that messed up.

Thank God I haven't stooped that low.

The show brought some comfort believing the age-old belief that God grades on the curve. At least, we concluded, we're not totally depraved.

Well, unfortunately, we are. *(Jeremiah 17:9)*.

We're just better at image management.

We grade by the wrong standard. Measured by God's law we're just as guilty as Jerry's guests. In Christ's light, we'd see the same darkness as theirs.

What's my point? Evil is lodged in our hearts too. I don't think we're so much better than them.

I remember driving by the Junior High school in our neighborhood and saying, "Nobody in there is doing well."

Actually, the same is true for adults.

It's why the only way we have a chance is God's intervention of grace thru the Cross, apart from our "good" works. *(Ephesians 2: 8-9)*.

The Bible calls my best behavior "filthy rags." *(Isaiah 64:6)*.

I'm not saying it's OK to travel down the wrong path. What I am saying is I have to stop comparing my behavior to others, then harshly judging them.

I can become a Jerry Springer Pharisee. "Well, at least I am not like one of those," says the JS Pharisee to the sinner..." *(Luke 18:11)*.

So easy to point the finger. Too easy to despise and dismiss. Reject and ridicule.

If my daily thoughts, words and actions were recorded on TV, my soap opera would make Jerry's madhouse look like a Disney cartoon.

Yours too?

# Bones

Imagine that you are a pall bearer and about to bury your best friend.

Then imagine minutes later you walk home with him.

That's exactly what happened in I Kings 13:31 in a dramatic, made for the movies scene when a dead Israelite touches the bones of Elisha the Prophet.

What in the world? Is this one of those Bible stories we just sail over, scratching our spiritual noggins?

The scene: Elisha, the ever active miracle working prophet, has just died. Placed into a tomb.

A bad gang of marauders come to town. The panicked pall bearers toss their friend in with Elisha: "When the body touched Elisha's bones. the man came to life and stood on his feet."

Nowhere else in the Bible does this happen. Is this hocus pocus superstition, like relics buried in church catacombs?

Of course not. But what does it mean?

In the Bible, bones refer to a place of power.

Specifically, God's power. Or lack of it.

Eighty four times bones are mentioned in Scripture. Like Adam describing Eve, "Bone of my bones." God's creative power.

When a marriage fails, the misery of it refers to rotting bones. When bones are healthy, it brings refreshment and delight.

Elisha seldom spoke. From Jericho's waters, raising the Shunamite's son, purifying a poisoned stew, feeding 100 men with a sack of grain... he acted in power.

So one last miracle came from his grave. The prophet is silenced. But God's power and promises never are.

When you least expect a miracle and need one, the God of the impossible brings a valley of dead bones to life. *(Ezekial 37)*.

Two thousand years ago, Someone else was placed in a tomb. But they did not crush His bones.

We read at the moment of His death, "The tombs broke open and the bodies of many holy people who had died were raised to life." *(Matthew 27:52)*.

We are all on a funeral march, about to be placed in our own graves. But when we are touched by Jesus we "come to life and stand on our feet".

Spiritual calcium for dry bones.

# New Beginnings

Did you know that the devout Hebrew lives by two calendars? Neither did I.

I discovered recently that Autumn ushers in their Tishri... which means The Beginning of the year.

But... Spring brings the Nisan which also means The Beginning.

So the Hebrew year has two beginnings, two calendars.

What gives?

The Fall is considered the secular start of the year.

Spring starts the sacred part of the year.

So what?

Just as the people of Israel live by two calendars, so does the Christian. The first calendar is natural; the second supernatural.

The first calendar: when we are born. The second: when we are born again. The moment we trust in Jesus Christ for eternal life.

Here's where it gets interesting to me.

When did the sacred calendar begin? At Jewish Passover. With the death of the Passover Lamb.

Messiah Jesus opens up the beauty of Spring.

Dreary winter gives way to the joy of Spring.

I remember as a kid hating winter… longing for the baseball season to begin.

Baseball Hall of Famer Rogers Hornsby, was asked what he does all winter, "I'll tell you what I do. I stare out the window and wait for spring."

I relate. As should all Believers. Eternal Spring is coming.

I loved the smell of the grass in Spring Training.

The rays of a warm sun in Florida. The feel of a brand new baseball. The laughter in the clubhouse.

For me, life began again.

I think Believers live with the same hope. Cold religion ends. Our Living Hope begins.

Every day we choose to live in the old calendar or the new one.

Grace vs. Law. Performance vs. acceptance. Life vs. death.

For the Believer, we die to ourselves in order to live for others. Life always comes out of death.

Just like our Jewish Messiah.

Spring forward or Fall back.

# Trains

Ever since I got a toy train set for Christmas at 10, I've always been fascinated by trains.

Whether riding a train through Europe, or enjoying the scenic route from Portland to Seattle, when given the time, give me the train.

My bucket list dream is to ride the Orient Express. Without the murder.

I don't think it's a stretch to say my Christian life is like a train.

There's the locomotive and all the railway cars it pulls. There are all kinds of engines: steam, diesel or electricity.

I get into trouble when the locomotive of my life pulls the box cars by emotions.

Emotions rule our sensuous culture: happiness, sadness, passivity, along with fear, anxiety and guilt. Just to name a few.

The problem comes when I make hasty decisions, measure my spiritual life, even doubt my salvation by emotions.

It always becomes a bumpy ride. Why? Feelings are real, just not reliable.

They help me appreciate the truth, but they don't reveal it. How I think determines my emotions. **(Proverbs 23:7)**.

The source of those thoughts? A mind empowered by faith in God's Word – the Bible. A powerful locomotive.

What is faith after all? Taking God at His Word.

Feelings are fickle, but God's Word is Forever.

I often feel like Jeremiah, the weeping prophet. His depressed sulking turns into delightful soaring when he remembers God's truth every morning.

God's mercies, compassions, faithfulness never budge. With no change in Jeremiah's circumstances, he tells his heart these truths. He goes from the outhouse to the penthouse. **(Lam. 3: 1-24)**.

Why is this so important? If you are feeling discouraged today– feel like God is far off, or doubt He loves you, your feelings have betrayed you.

If you are feeling unforgiven by God or uncertain about your future, your emotions are driving the train. Feelings have their place– in the caboose.

Here's the point: don't trust your heart. Inform it.

The Engineer will keep you on track.

# Limping

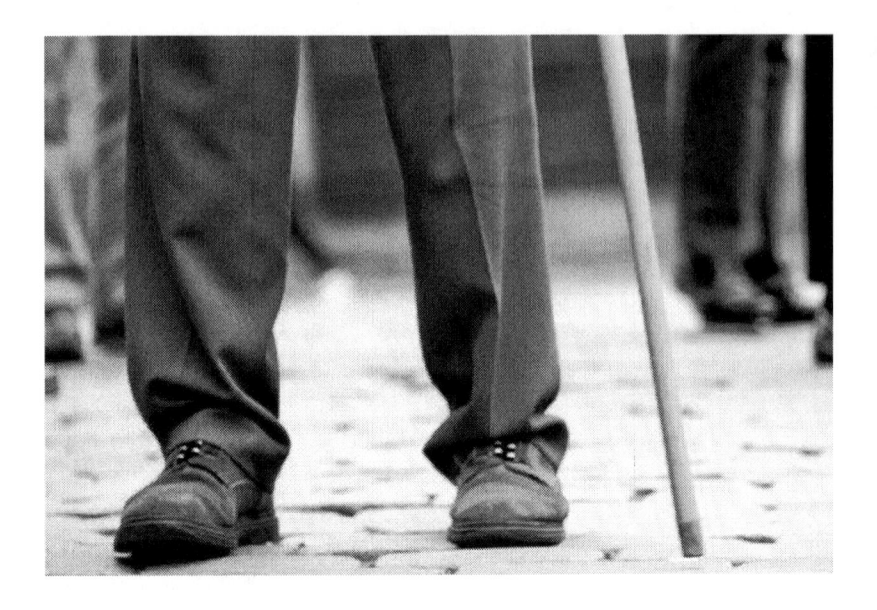

On Memorial Day I fell and fractured my hip.

Limping in from the front yard, I knew my life had changed.

This morning my hip aches. Some days are better than others.

But this annoying hip is a good thing. It reminds me of God's grace. How so?

My limp got me thinking about one of my least favorite characters, Jacob of the Old Testament.

Turns out he's like me.

Not because I wrestled with God and got pinned. I tripped over a hose watering flowers for goodness sakes.

Here's the deal...

Adults we thought were heroes as kids, we discovered, are not. Especially in the Bible.

Sunday School material paints portraits like Noah the Obedient or David the Brave. Those are half-truths at best.

Biblical characters, like Christians today and in every generation, have skeletons in their closets, dark basements in their hearts.

The Scripture gives saints with clay feet their moments of valor, but also ugliness in lurid color- for millennia to see.

Raw, even evil motives have become sermon material for hundreds of years. Lord, deliver me from such fame.

I love CS Lewis classic comment, "What? You too? I thought I was the only one." The truth is we are far from alone.

We are all flawed and frail. This gives me hope. Our wise God chooses imperfect people like Jacob to encourage me.

Jacob fights to be #1 in the womb. He lies. He plays favorites. He is an unfair opportunist. Takes advantage of others.

And he fights with God.

God doesn't try to pretty up His man of deceit. He gives him a limp. But in the end, OT believers even adopted his new name: Israel.

Jesus didn't pick the 12 best. God doesn't pick the pious or the devout to change the world.

As a friend said to me, "God pans for gold in the sewers of this world. He finds stinky rocks that he washes and polishes with grace."

Jacob limped for the rest of his life. We all have aching hips. God gave me a perfect memorial on Memorial Day.

My limp reminds me that the longer I follow Him, the weaker I become, and the more I lean on His Grace.

I think I will discover that in the end, I never limped at all: He carried me every step of the way.

Like Jacob.

Like me.

Like you.

# University of the Cross

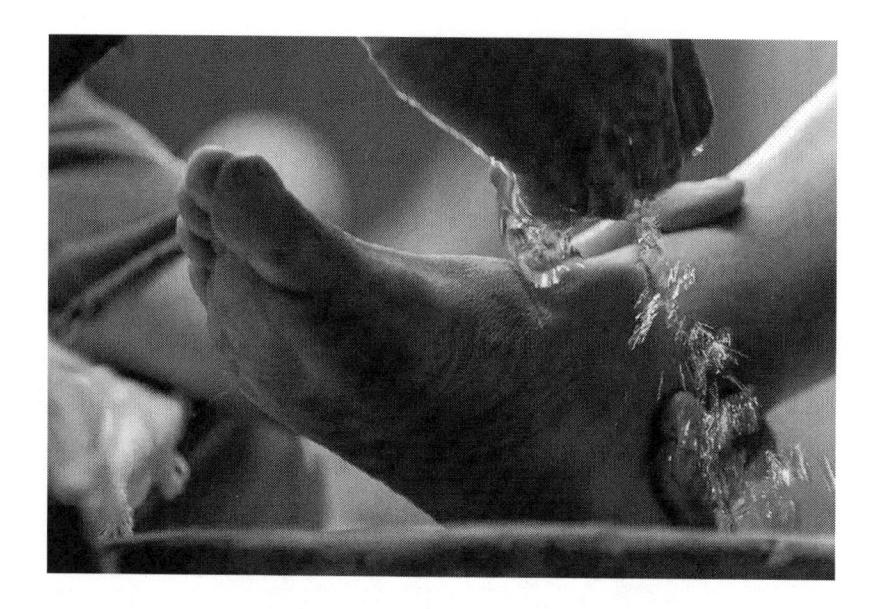

Be first. Be the best. Be somebody. Stand out. Rise above. Dream big.

Be anything but normal.

The sirens of our culture. For so many years, I bought the lie.

Looking back, here's what I now think: there is much contentment in dreaming small.

Let's read from the man who wrote two-thirds of the New Testament at the end of his life, "Make it your ambition to lead a quiet life." **(I Thessalonians 4:11)**.

In other words, make it your ambition to not be ambitious.

Make it your ambition to not drink our Christian cultural's Kool-aid.

Bluntly put, I think there is real joy in an unaccomplished life. Don't let your personal glory be the bling of your bio.

To lead a quiet life doesn't mean we lower our expectations. It means we lower our eyes. Looking beside us, looking around us. Seeing what's in front of us.

And find our Savior in the most unexpected places. I think Jesus hides beneath His opposite.

He is not out to be impressive. When it comes time to praise the first, He exalts the last.

Somewhere in my faith journey I lost my way. I got wrapped up in ambitious dreams. Teach at a seminary, pastor a church, write a book, get one degree after another.

I could quote Augustine but couldn't name my kids favorite toy. I was just chasing idols. The next trophy, The most Incredible!, awesome! unbelievable! experience.

The next "big thing."

My favorite quote these days, "Our greatest fear should not be failure, but in succeeding at something that doesn't really matter."

I hope it's not too late for my blinders to be ripped off: To see a Jesus that walked with the heartbroken, washed dirty feet, visited the imprisoned, emptied His veins as others mocked.

Not bigger, bolder, better. But rather the Lord of the lowly. Gentle of heart.

There is nothing glittering about serving an exhausted mother, a hungry neighbor, a needy child. Except to God who sees all.

Ordinary faithfulness is the main subject taught at the University of the Cross. Turns out it's not very ordinary.

The major? Meeting needs more important than our own **(Philippians 2:3)**.

So now my burning ambition?

To not have one.

# Light vs. Darkness

I am leaving for Poland tonight. A long trip for me: back just before Thanksgiving.

As I have seen the War in Ukraine morph over the last eight plus months, I draw one huge conclusion: the first casualty of war is the truth.

It has moved from the insane to the bizarre. The leadership in Russia has lost their collective minds.

If it weren't for the atrocities and loss of lives, it would be Theatre of the Absurd. Now it is Theatre of the Tragic.

Putin's shifting strategy: de-Nazify the Ukrainians even though President Zalensky is a Jew, to freezing civilians out in the upcoming winter.

How?

By destroying 40% of Ukraine's energy infrastructure.

The latest? Declaring his war is a Holy War: with Russia the Christians and Ukrainians the satanists.

Upside down logic at its worst. It is the work of the Devil alright. Just reverse the roles.

The "angel of light" *(2 Corinthians 11:14)* who came to seek and destroy is working his black magic. And the despicable thing is many of the Russian people are buying the lies.

Just yesterday I received a Twitter video of an annual Lviv celebration featuring "hundreds of people marching for a Nazi Gestapo unit".

Turns out it's Ukrainians marching for their heroes who bravely defended a city in Ukraine in this unjust war.

And if you didn't know the Ukrainian language, you might think, "See there! Nazi sympathizers." Infuriating.

So let me ask you a question: Do you honestly think Russia will stop their aggression if they win this war? Think again. Russia has been barbaric for decades.

My opinion: if it weren't for politics, NATO could send the Russians back to Moscow, tail between it's legs, in two days.

I am admittedly fiercely loyal to the Ukrainians, having been going there to see the will of this resolute nation since 2010. But loyalty hasn't blinded me to the truth.

My biggest ache as a Christian: that lives can be hurled into eternity without a faith in the only One who can win the War of the Soul.

I am only one person. But I serve a living God who is not asleep at the wheel. He does not take sides. He takes over.

Wars have been a constant since Eden. There will one day be another one so horrible that blood will rise to the bridles of horses. *(Revelation 14:20)*.

It may be soon. Only coming King Jesus on His White Stallion know.

While the time may be short, you and I have today. Redeem it.

We will win in the end. Until then, we fight on. Please pray and fight with me.

Slava Ukrayini.

P.S. The photo with this Salt Talk is real. It is a photo of an Azovstal defender named Orest, recently released from Russian captivity. It received first prize at the International Photography Contest.

# Upside Down

At age 30, I had my life pretty well mapped out.

Graduate school was finished, and I had truth labeled in tiny black and white boxes.

Tough questions were answered with a variety of Biblical proof-texts. With perhaps a slight smugness in tone.

I was pastoring, writing, going to the mission field, and soon teaching at a conservative, buttoned up seminary.

That was 45 years ago.

Today, met with questions I can't answer, I'd probably say, "Let's get a beer and talk about it."

Somewhere in that conversation, I'd talk about Truth named Jesus.

If I never got around to Him, we'd just be two beer-drinking philosophers kicking back on a Saturday night.

The one who is the Way, the Truth and the Life is the only person who can tell you what really matters. **(John 14:6)**.

And if you follow Him, He will turn your life upside down in the best and most uncomfortable ways.

Impossible-to-describe ways.

Early Christians were falsely accused. Nero blamed them for burning Rome down in AD 64. Tacitus said they practiced abominations. Most said they believed a perverted superstition.

But there was one accusation leveled at Christians that was true. It wasn't meant to be a compliment.

Their opponents claimed the Jesus followers had "turned the world upside down." **(Acts 17:6)**.

Jesus Himself was the culprit. He didn't just color outside the lines. He flips over the paper and re-paints us.

His work doesn't make sense. It wasn't designed to.

Jesus turns our world upside down with what The Bible calls "the foolishness of God." **(I Corinthians 1:25)**.

Q and A...

How do you save your life? Jesus: By losing it.

How do you become the greatest? Jesus: By being the least.

How do you get ahead? Jesus: By putting others first.

Turned upside down. Jesus is always turning our world upside down to slowly put it right side up.

# Freedom

Nobody has just one calling in life.

To say work is our calling is like equating a tire with a car. It's only one slice of the pie.

A vocation is not only how we make a living. It's how life has made us. Are you a son or daughter, mom or dad, husband or wife, boss or employee?

On April 8, 1947 I was called to be a son, brother and an American. Still in diapers and God had called me to 3 vocations.

Now? Christ Follower, Husband, Father, Grandfather, Speaker.

Why is this so important?

Our world pounds away at us about the importance of finding our calling. Here's what I think…

Failing to find "your calling" is actually good news.

Because it's a waste of time. You can't dig it up, because it's not buried.

It's not a deep mystery. No need to wait for the heavens to part. They won't.

Rather, just look around. Our calling is as clear as the face of our neighbor.

We could spend hours going to Job Fairs. Looking for the dot in the Divine Decree. Trying to find our spiritual Waldo.

He has given us no instruction as to what skill to acquire, which career path to choose, who to marry.

He has left us free to choose.

I think God is just as happy if you choose to be a cop or an oral surgeon. A congressman or a repairman.

Just short of a divine shrug, I don't think it matters much to God.

Wanna be a rocket scientist? Very cool. Wanna drive a truck coast to coast? Nice choice.

How we love our parents, our children, our customers, our friends, our enemies is what counts. These are our callings.

We all go through crossroads: should I sell cars, become a priest, be a janitor or jeweler? Teach kids at school? Train them at home?

Here's my answer: God doesn't care the way we think He does.

He only cares if you seek first His Kingdom and its righteousness. *(Matthew 6:33)*.

Because He will give you everything else. Seek Him first and every vocation is blessed.

This has a big payoff: it sets us free. No introspection, no wondering "did I miss it?" You won't.

Turns out "love God and do as you please" is great advice **(Ps. 37:4)**.

God isn't playing Hide and Go Seek.

Only Seek and He Won't Hide.

# Recalibrating

There were two fish swimming along, and happened to meet an older fish swimming the other way.

He nods at the two, and says, "Morning, boys, How's the water?"

The two young fish swim on for awhile, and then suddenly, one looks at the other and says, "What the hell is water?"

I have a friend who constantly uses the word recalibrate. I cannot get that word out of my mind this morning.

It collides with something a radical guy named Paul said, "Do not be conformed to this world, but be transformed by the renewing of your mind." **(Romans 12:2)**.

I've been told that the word "conformed" means to be "squeezed into its mold." Our cultural waters are squeezing us tighter and tighter.

And it has become such a part of our reality, so natural, so all consuming we rarely pause to ask, "What the hell is water?"

Recalibrate. How?

..."that by testing (the waters) you may discern the will of God: good, acceptable and perfect."

So I must ask two questions, "How's the water?"

"What does Jesus say about it?" Then recalibrate.

It's always a choice.

If I'm not careful, I swim so long in the water I don't redirect.

Instead, I redefine–my own sin. I give rebellion a holy name.

I actually call my wilderness wanderings a kind of righteousness.

Narcissism becomes ambition.

Greed becomes wise business decisions.

Slander becomes just telling the truth.

On and on it goes. I am guilty of it. We all are. Why?

Because we seldom ask the question: How's my water?

After all, how could we fish live without it?

I'd have to become a fish out of water. Maybe jump into Living Water.

Exactly.

# In Search of Sasquatch

If you're married, both of you know you don't complete each other.

That would be impossible, unrealistic and a burden no person is capable of bearing.

But countless couples have crazy expectations of their husband or wife, "Give me comfort, give me edge. Give me novelty, give me familiarity. Give me predictability, give me surprise."

Let's be honest. That's not asking each other to be a spouse. It's asking them to be a god.

Finding our soulmate will happen when we see the Loch Ness Monster riding a Unicorn. Our search for Sasquatch.

Sooner or later we discover that the only candidates available for marriage are sinners.

Every last one of us. Two ticks in search of a dog. But let's not be so cynical. Let's dare to dream a little. Imagine a marriage where one spouse makes the other person perfect, totally complete.

Here's the truth: there's no imagining to it. No fantasy required. It's already happened. It's exactly who we are in Jesus. We are His Bride.

He is the Husband of our souls. The irony: if there is one message we offer to a confused world it's this...we've already married the only Ideal Spouse.

Believers are a a part of His beloved bride, called the church.

While our world urges us to seek another person to be content, we have Jesus. He's enough.

No newlywed happiness that melts over time, but a secure hope even in our darkest days. No Valentine's Day.

Instead we have Easter Day. We discover marriage is a gift from God wrapped in a Cross.

As one person puts it, "Marriage is the round hole for our square-shaped hearts. It's the training ground that teaches love and self-sacrifice are synonymous."

If all this comes across as anti-Disney and annoyingly pessimistic, I'm sorry. I just think it's plain old reality.

Neither cheerful or depressing. It's the way things are in a fallen and fractured world.

Here's my point: If our marital wisdom comes from Netflix or Nashville, self-help books or even some churches, illusion turns into disillusionment. Fast.

Bottom line: There is no Mr. or Ms. Right. Stop the search.

As my pre-marriage counselor said almost 50 years ago, "Never hope to find a perfect woman."

Of course I asked, "Why not?"

His response? "If she's perfect, she won't need you."

# Mountains

I was the oldest to ever go on an insane mountain climbing trip.

To my knowledge, I still win the geriatrics award. At 70, I flew to Colorado to be stripped of my watch, my phone, and my dignity. Add to that any common sense.

Seven of us were going to climb in the Rocky Mountains for five days. I must have had altitude sickness BEFORE I signed up.

It was sobering. The most disturbing part? Our guides gave us no idea when we'd stop or where we were going.

The most insane part? I actually paid for this torture. It was both humiliating, life changing, with a mixture of beauty and brutality.

It was almost as good as thinking I could fly like Superman when I was 11 and broke my arm. The flight was fun. The landing not so much.

The idea of mountain climbing sounded fun. The experience? If you like flies, feel like Daniel Boone but look like Pee Wee Herman, and enjoy eating out of a tin can, it was a memory maker.

This adventure in futility reminded me of my Christian life.

If you're like me, you are exhilarated by a vision of your future self- like ascending a mountain and breathlessly reaching the top.

Only to become aware of your flaws and failures.

Feel your struggles.Repeat your stumbles.

I had visions of grandeur back in 2017, sorta like Rocky thrusting his fists in the air at the summit.

Not even close.

Just like now at 75, climbing towards Jesus, I'm very aware of my lingering rebellion. In fact, the older I get, my stubborn habits root like weeds.

The irony: the higher up the mountain I climbed in Colorado, the farther away the peak seemed.

There were days when I thought "I'll never get there." Just like my faith. Today I just hope I can keep a few of His commandments with fewer embarrassing falls.

On my 5 days of reckoning, I had this thought: My Christian life has never been a smooth trail to the top.

My faith in Jesus isn't so much about me ascending but about God descending.

Just like at Bethlehem, the Son of God came down the mountain to save us because we couldn't save ourselves.

We climb because He is our Life. He bids us on.

We rest because He is our Mercy. He knows our frame.

He also made the mountain.

# Innkeepers

I think doubt gets a bad rap.

I have never thought it was faith OR doubt for the Christian. I think Its has always been faith AND doubt.

One cannot live without the other.

If I took some money, hid it in my hand, and asked, "Do you think I have money hidden here?"

You might say yes, believing me by faith.

When I open my hand and produce a $20 bill, I have just destroyed your faith. Why?

Because you now have complete knowledge. No need for faith. You know for certain.

We now "see through a glass darkly." We do not have complete certainty. Let's call that doubt.

There are two kinds of doubt: dishonest and honest. The first is lazy and riddled with disdain.

It's deemed impossible or stupid.

It rejects real thinking. It walks away.

But honest doubt prompts questions. It is humble and vulnerable.

Just like Thomas. John the Baptist. Peter. Elijah. Gideon. Moses. David. Jonah.

And yes, just like the Mother of Jesus.

Mary, a poor 14 year old hears some startling news. From an angel no less. "You will give birth to the Savior of the World." **(Luke 1: 35)**.

But, she protests, "How can these things be, since I am a virgin?"

There's always doubt before courage. Suspicion before surrender.

I find odd comfort that Mary was troubled by the news. Pondered it, and wondered how it could be. We all ponder, feel troubled and wonder why me at times.

Gabriel then gives one of the greatest assurances in all of the Bible: "Nothing is impossible with God."

Without Mary's doubt, the angel would have never uttered those words which have comforted Christians for centuries.

Mary's faith, spilling out right after deep doubt, suddenly fuels her commitment, "I am the Lord's servant, may it be to me as you have said." **(Luke 1:38)**.

Commitment is far different than certainty.

Honest doubt leaves room for the impossible.

Dishonest doubt leaves no room at all.

At the first Christmas, there was no room at the Inn. Ultimately, we're all just Innkeepers.

Honest doubt always makes room for Jesus.

The No Vacancy sign is off.

# Going in Circles

Christmas was a riot at our house. Twenty bodies: 12 kids and 8 adults trying to hold it together.

The inmates definitely took over the asylum.

Adults bumped into one another with dazed looks.

We set up a numbering system like Baskin Robbins to take short order requests during meals.

We were like a concierge in search of a tip.

Breathless and happy.

Its caused me to think about circles. As in Whirling Dervish Circles.

I was watching an episode of "The Chosen" recently and the scene was at the Wedding of Cana.

I noticed that the disciples, the wedding guests and yes, Jesus were dancing–in circles.

It was pure joy...laughter, unbridled celebration. Holy gyrations. I found myself grinning like a Cheshire Cat.

Such exuberance.

I discovered that the dance had a name in Hebrew: the Khag. The Dance of the Circles.

We have just experienced a Dance of the Circles: Christmas... a Holy Day, a festival of celebration, not unlike Easter.

A time to rejoice and be glad! The King has come. But here's the interesting twist: the whole earth was created to Dance the Khag. Notice the wonder of sunrise and sunset as our earth spins.

It's a Circle Dance around the sun. The man in the moon smiles. The stars dance with a dazzling rhythm.

I know Believers will dance in heaven. I wouldn't be surprised if millions will Circle Dance around the throne.

Yes, the world is a mess in 2022. We can choose to grovel and lament about our unraveling world.

Or we can dance.

January 1 marks another trip around the sun. A circle completed. We can either sit on the sidelines and scowl–or join the dance.

I remember clearly at Lenexa Grade School the ones who had fun were the dancers. They broke the ice from "boys go with boys... girls go with girls."

They got up, joined the circle, and danced.

At my age, it's easier to sit it out. My resolution for 2023 is to join the Khag.

A celebration of the Lord, an act of unrestrained worship, a festival of His love, a sacred expression of joy!

Turn up the music Christians. The world will notice.

May I have this dance?

Let's get dizzy.

# Sleep

I crave a good night's sleep.

But I think the whole world is suffering from sleep deprivation.

I'm out early on New Year's day. Nobody's on the streets. I'm alone in my little coffee shop at 7 a.m.

I have been up for 2.5 hours and its been crickets.

After the chaos of Christmas and a mandatory "Happy New Year!" at midnight... the world seems eerily quiet.

Asleep. But are we resting?

I believe grace determines everything spiritually.

Sleep is nipping right at its heels for second place.

I go to bed at 9:30; up at 4:30. I have never really believed "early to bed, early to rise makes a man healthy, wealthy and wise."

I'm poor, have a limp, and remain a mess. I do believe in this cliche: Fatigue makes cowards of us all.

I find it fascinating how I trust God and how I love others are determined largely by my sleep... or lack of it.

I will stay up later for a good friend, get up early to make an airport run. Admire parents bleary eyed due to their newborns.

Or I will wrestle through the night fretting about my work or health. I'll toss and turn because I can't solve a problem.

Here's what I think: Our hearts are often raw at the end of a long day. We decide whether to trust or love. Sleep provides the fuel.

Ultimately, apart from a physical issue, I think our sleep problems may point to a spiritual problem.

Psalm 127 reads, "Unless the Lord watches over the City, the watchman stays awake in vain. He gives to his beloved sleep."

As the song says, "We're fighting a battle He's already won. We may not know what He's doing, but we know what He's done."

Sleep is a gift. Being anxious is a curse.

Instead of New Years Resolutions, why not make some Restolutions.

The Bible says God works even when we sleep. He neither sleeps nor slumbers. ***(Psalm 21:4-5)***.

We rest easy while He works beautifully.

Birds of the air and Lilies of the field have figured it out. ***(Matthew 6)***.

Sweet Dreams in 2023.

# Certain Doubt

I think the most fascinating guy in the Bible is John the Baptist.

You've got to admire a renegade who snacks on locusts, and washes them down with wild honey.

Fearless and bold, this preacher would never win a popularity contest.

Yet Jesus said of him, "Of those born of women there has arisen no one greater than John the Baptist."

This rugged prophet, the first since Malachi in 400 years, was a walking miracle from the start.

When Gabriel announced to Mary that she would give birth to the Messiah, the angel also talked about John.

Saying he would be leap in Elizabeth's womb at the mere sound of Mary's voice who carried the Christ child.

John would reluctantly baptize Jesus after announcing he was not worthy to untie the sandals of the Messiah.

Yet one of the greatest men who ever lived died in doubt, beheaded by Herod's hateful revenge.

John had asked the disciples to go fetch the One who could stop his awful death. Yet Jesus did not come.

No rescue of his friend, no sympathy note. Jesus actually tells his men to tell John He was busy performing miracles.

And John's honest response: "Are you really the Messiah, or should we look for another?"

Notice Jesus doesn't get angry at his question.

Instead, He continues, tell John: "I am healing the sick, giving sight to the blind, cleansing lepers, restoring the deaf." **(Luke 7)**.

Really?

I don't know about you, but I would feel rejected and hurt. As if my best Friend had better things to do.

Doesn't He owe John? Evidently not. His head on Herod's platter gives me a clue.

While I admit John's death is puzzling, I conclude with two truths– since I believe Jesus is always good and always loving.

First, honest doubt is not a loss of faith. Second, we only know in part. His ways are unfathomable, past finding out.

Judging Divine Motives is dangerously prideful. And doubt is inevitable.

At times, we all feel like John: a "lone voice crying in the wilderness." Life will bring you to your knees.

God does hears. God will answer. But in His time, not mine.

I believe John's reward awaited. And so does ours.

Keep crying.

# Scandalous

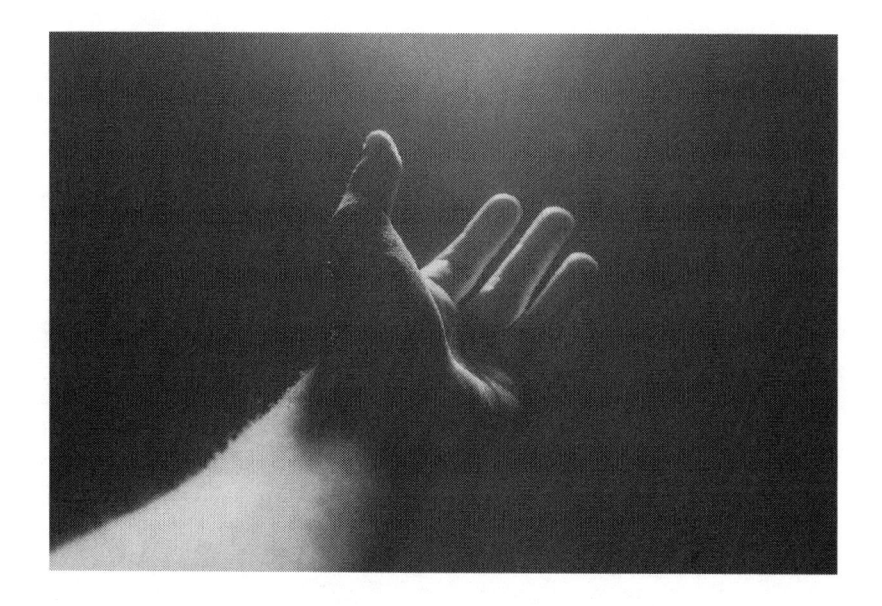

Agnostics, skeptics, hardened criminals shed tears when they hear it. Me too.

The song: Amazing Grace.

Nothing is as stunning as God's grace.

If grace seems less than amazing, less full of wonder, we really don't understand grace.

The great Puritan preacher, Jonathan Edwards, put it this way, "Grace is but Glory begun, and Glory is but Grace perfected."

The problem is we've grown accustomed to using the word and failed to be astounded by it.

It should shock us. But are we awestruck?

As one person put it, "The ultimate test of our spirituality is the measure of our amazement at the Grace of God."

I wholeheartedly agree.

I used to think I have failed God so often, I am unworthy of Grace. THIS time? Not again. Guilty.

Ashamed. Beat myself up.

But that very unworthiness moved a new Christian named John Newton, a slave trader, to write his classic hymn.

"Amazing Grace- how sweet the sound- that saved a wretch like me."

We don't deserve it; we can't earn it. **(Ephesians 2: 8-9)**.

Grace begins when we realize we owe God everything; He owes us nothing.

In a London conference on comparative religions, scholars debated on what belief was unique to the Christian faith. The debate raged until C.S. Lewis walked into the room.

"That's easy," Lewis said, "It's grace."

Here's the good news: we cannot earn what we cannot lose. We cannot stop getting grace since we never deserved it in the first place.

The problem is that grace offends our human pride...our independence. We try to add something to the Gift.

Here's the truth. If we don't see how utterly broken and undeserving we are, God's grace won't seem so amazing.

Grace is the opposite of what the world says is important.

We simply cling to the Cross. "Nothing in my hand I bring, simply to the cross I cling."

Shocking, sweet, scandalous Grace.

Jesus went through hell to give it. We bow a knee to receive it.

More than amazing.

# Fences

When: World War II.

Where: A remote village in the countryside of France.

During an intense battle, an American soldier is killed.

His comrades retrieve his body and knowing he was an outspoken Believer, want to give him a Christian burial.

They recall seeing a small church a few miles down the road behind the front lines.

They remember a small cemetery surrounded by a white fence.

Getting permission to move the body, they arrive at the church just before sunset.

Knocking on the door of the church, an old priest opens the door.

"Our friend was killed in battle," one soldier said, "and we want to give him a Christian burial."

Speaking very little English, the priest still understood, but said, "I'm very sorry, but we can bury only those of the same faith here."

The weary soldiers, disappointed but hardened by many months of war, turn to walk away. "But," said the priest, "you can bury him outside the fence."

Exhausted and cynical, the soldiers dig a grave and bury their friend outside the white fence.

It's way past nightfall before they finish.

The next morning, as the entire unit moved on, many of his friends race back to say one final goodbye to their friend.

But when they arrive they can't find his gravesite. Confused and angry, they knock on the door of the priest.

They ask the priest if he knows where they have buried their friend. "It was dark and we were so tired last night. We must have been disoriented."

The old priest pauses and says, "After you left last night, I could not sleep. So I went outside early this morning and moved the fence."

Until Jesus came, we were all outside the fence of God's love.

But now there is nothing we can do to stop God from loving us.

"Nothing can separate us from the love of God." **(Romans 8:38-39)**.

Nothing.

Jesus did more than move the fence. He tore it down.

# Good Luck

A Godly friend called me the other day and asked me one question: "Do you believe in luck?"

I've been thinking about it ever since.

I told him I didn't Biblically, but I do say it to others.

Probably the better word for the Believer is Blessing....the kind that comes through God's filtered Hand.

But here's the question I have: can we stir God's heart to give us one?

I may be skating on spiritual thin ice here, but I think we can.

I often hear how a marriage is past fixing, or a prodigal kid will never change. People have a will of their own we reason.

We cannot fix things. But God can and does radically change hearts.

From Pharaoh's heart to Paul's Damascus, God can and does intervene with His awesome power.

Have you seen Him give a Blessing that is supernatural, inexplicable, miraculous?

I believe there is a better way to move our mountain. Call it God's good luck. Directly from Him. He calls it inheriting a Blessing.

In 1986, at a family reunion, Kathy and I decided to give a blessing to each of our three young children.

We searched the Old Testament. We saw the power of giving a Blessing to inherit a Divine one.

With the five of us gathered, each child was seated alone at the front. Whitney, then John, then Mindy.

We talked about their remarkable qualities. We spoke well of each child. We gave a eulogy.

We then told each child what we hoped for their future. A Godly mate, an impact for Jesus, a life of overcoming evil with good.

And finally, we all gathered around each child, laid hands on them, prayed for them. Asked God to pour out His Blessing on them.

We then summarized our words to each. Gave them a life verse of Scripture. Made a laminated copy of it all, dated it.

I have no doubt that God has accomplished all that we asked that day.

I believe He is waiting to give His unique Blessing to you. He shares this kind of Glory with no one.

All our therapy groups, rehab clinics, and books are helpful. But only God performs the heart miracle.

Invoking His sovereign, providential Blessing the Biblical way is so often ignored. Unleash it.

I don't believe in Good Luck. But I do believe in Great Blessing.

HIs.

# Eulogies

The sand of life is running faster through my hourglass.

It's sobering to realize the number of people who attend our funerals will be largely determined by the weather.

I've been thinking about the difference between CV virtues and Eulogy virtues.

CV virtues are professional and buttoned up. They point to comparison of others. Eulogy virtues are spiritual, and require no comparison.

Eulogy virtues are what people say about you at funerals.

He was a loving father vs. all conference QB at Podunk University.

In reality, it was hard to focus on eulogy virtues when I was young. It just didn't feel all that special.

I could easily be distracted from being, well, just plain nice.

At almost 76, I've lost my edge on some CV skills. Diminished capacity to perform. Not as sharp. You know, slowing down.

People I've talked to at the end of their careers wistfully tell me how they want to be remembered. I suppose we all do.

But here's the problem: they won't. They'll forget you. They move on.

Take the movie "About Schmidt", starring Jack Nicholson. He's a hard working actuary, about to retire.

But in the days after his retirement, he is saddened as he drops by his old office to help. No one wants his advice.

In fact, he finds them throwing his old work in the dumpster.

We wince in empathy, but realize it's the truth. For all of us.

One person put it this way, "In just six months I went from "Who's Who" to "Who's He?"

C.S. Lewis said it best. "Never let your happiness depend on something you can lose."

When the Apostle Paul listed all of his CV virtues in Philippians 3, he compared them to manure. Why?

Because, he says, he put his brag sheet next to the surpassing greatness of knowing Christ. His Eulogy Virtue. No comparison.

I've never heard of a man on his death bed wanting to take one last ride in his Tesla. Or total up his 401K.

I have heard eulogies marked by love, joy, peace, patience, kindness, goodness, faithfulness, gentleness, self-control as they followed Jesus. *(Galatians 5:22)*.

Heaven's Eulogy.

# Waiting

I love the game of baseball. I always have, always will.

From T-ball to the Major Leagues, I am one happy man at the ballpark.

Spring Training is about to begin. I can't wait to spit sunflower seeds, smell hot dogs and green grass, hear the crack of the bat.

The seventh inning stretch, singing Deep in the Heart of Texas, replays on the Jumbotron, even the outdated Wave... give me ALL of it.

But, strange as it may seem, what I like most about baseball is the pace.

It's a slow game. While many say baseball is boring, I say it's my therapy.

In a world of spinning plates and hurry up to keep up, my baseball addiction stands still. It stubbornly refuses to play hurried.

Here's what I like about it the most: it forces me to wait. It's even called our past time. It is waaay past time. In the best sort of way.

You wait for your turn in the batting order. You wait for the ball to be hit to you. You wait for the pitcher to warm up. You wait between innings.

And most importantly you wait for your pitch.

Baseball is the only sport of the Big Four: Baseball, Football, Basketball, Hockey that doesn't have a time clock.

In baseball you wait for everything. They keep trying to hurry the game up. Baseball will have none of it.

But... when the action comes, you best get ready. You have .25 seconds when your pitch comes. The crack of the bat may send the baseball screaming at 100 MPH.

I can hear my dad still telling me, "Wait for your pitch." He taught me how to hit. He taught me patience... along with the best tutor... the game I love.

Nine innings are defiant. A holy sports grail. We would never leave until the very last out.

Our modern pace isn't strong enough to knock baseball out of the park. From my Lenexa Kansas little leagues, to the Kansas City Royals, baseball taught me to wait.

With grandkids, I admonish to wait for your pitch. From one generation to another, we are taught that good things come to those who wait.

Our God also instructs us as well too: "Wait on Me", He says. He shows us He's never in a hurry, but always on time.

It's not easy to wait. I don't like it. I swing at bad pitches. I'm fooled by a hard breaking curve. Bamboozled by a sneaky change of pace.

But I believe my pitch will come. So will yours. It only takes one swing to hit a grand slam.

The best piece of advice I ever received came from a baseball coach:

"There is only one thing worse than waiting," he said. And what was that?

Wishing you had.

# Carried

When I was a youngster, I loved to play possum.

My parents would go to a friends home, put me to bed early, and play a card game called Pinochle.

I would doze, or pretend to.

I would be in and out of sleep. Inevitably, they would finish, and I would fake sleep.

All because I wanted to be carried by my dad.

Out to the car, gently placed in the back seat of their 1951 Ford, my world was as it should be.

But the best was ahead. Still flopping with my limp body, my dad would climb the steps to our tiny apartment in Kansas City.

My mom would come in, pat my face, kiss me on the cheek, pull up the covers.

I would fall into a peaceful slumber.

Like a security blanket, I still want that. But as I go through the Golden Years, I look to a different Carrier.

In Isaiah 46, there is a passage of Scripture that is deeply comforting. It was read at my Father-in-Law's 100th Birthday Party.

"Listen to me. Carried from the womb, even to your old age I am He. And to gray hairs I will carry you. I will carry you and will save."

Carry me and save me.

Yes, He cares for all of us. **(I Peter 5:7)** But my spirit leaps when I think Jesus' care is translated into being carried. So tender.

Not the fiery King of Kings returning on His white horse. Not the Lion of Judah. Not the One who stops Armageddon in its tracks.

But it's the Lamb of God who carries me. Carries you. The one Who weeps over all of us.

The Bible refers to death as sleep. Can you imagine what it will be like to fall asleep and wake up in His Arms? I picture it. I want it.

At 75, it is easy to be fearful as I face crossing the Veil. I am not afraid. I long for the day I will live with both the Lion and the Lamb.

Strong enough to protect me; gentle enough to carry me.

Jesus will one day cover me up with his grace, pat my childlike face with love, and comfort me with a holy kiss.

Tucked in for eternity.

# Why?

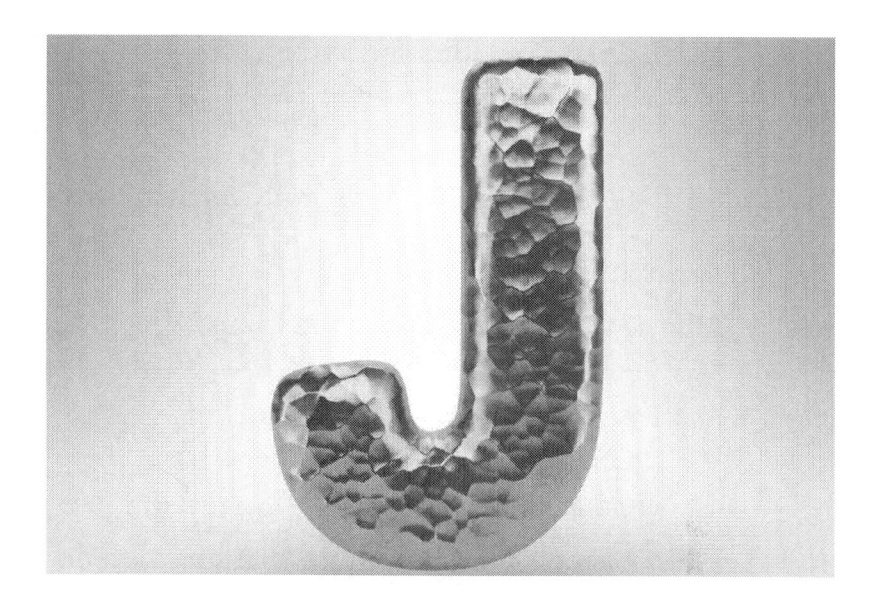

Where is God when it hurts?

It's the question that never goes away.

The atrocities against Ukraine. The death of a child. And the scores of other questions that end in "Why?"

If He's an all powerful, always loving God–what gives?

Let's face it: nobody has an answer that satisfies the heart.

The first physician to die of AIDS in England was a young Christian who caught the disease conducting medical research in Africa.

In the last days, he struggled to speak.

Near the end, unable to talk, he had just enough strength to scribble one letter to his wife.

The letter J.

She went through her mental rolodex, giving words that started with J. None were right. Finally she said, "Jesus?"

He nodded. Yes, Jesus.

Jesus was all he wanted to say. It was all she needed to hear.

In the end, all the questions asking "why" won't matter. Even if I knew the answer, it wouldn't ease the pain.

All our answers fall short. At times they even sound cold, canned, bookish.

None give me peace.

No comforting answer to why babies die of SIDS. No answer to ease Turkey's earthquake toll. On and on.

I don't need an explanation. I need a Person.

Jesus: "In ME you have peace." **(John 14:27)**.

There is only One Name who brings peace too deep for words. Truth that passes understanding. One who transcends the whys?

His Name begins with J.

# One Word

I love the power of words.

One story. One sentence. Even one word can change your life.

Proverbs says "Life and death are in the power of the tongue."

What do you think is the single most Important word ever spoken?

I am convinced it is a Greek word: Tetelestai.

It was an ancient word used when someone met the terms of a contract.

Tetelestai would be stamped on a bill of sale. It meant that a debt had been "paid in full".

Tetelestai was the final word that Jesus Christ uttered on the Cross before He died.

The translation? "It is finished."

My work is done.

The Greek word is a tense not known in the English language (the past perfect). It means an action taken place in the past that's still going on today.

In other words, the Savior of the World was saying "it was paid by Me then... and I will continue paying today."

What exactly did He purchase? Us. It's the Easter Story.

Resurrection Sunday proclaims that Jesus took on the sin of the world – past, present and future. Paid for it with His blood.

In the end, God the Father will open two scrolls at the final judgment: the Book of Life and the Book of Works.

Our names are written in one of those Books. Good works never measure up. Only Tetelestai opens the other.

The Good News? There is no Book of Sin. Our sin is never mentioned. Jesus took care of it.

When we believe the Promise of Jesus *(John 3:16)*.

God writes our names in the Book of Life. Never to be erased. Permanent marker. Indelible red ink.

On Good Friday Jesus gave the most amazing, victorious promise ever made.

You're fighting a battle I've already won.

It is finished!

# Words of Comfort

I was deep in the heart of Nigeria when I got the news. It trickled in slowly.

There was one computer in the entire village and it ran two hours a day by generator. If you were lucky.

The news of our oldest grandson's birth came in spurts. At first, it's a boy!

Then sober news: his breathing is labored. Then... he's in NICU.

I was staying in the home of a Bishop whose last name I could never pronounce.

He saw the anguish on my face. He sat down beside me and said nothing. Put his hand on my shoulder.

And still said nothing.

In due time, I spilled my anxious thoughts. He finally said, "Thank you for sharing this with me."

I blubbered out some more worry.

He paused and said, "This is really a difficult situation."

Still more silence followed…and then the five words that made me feel so loved.

"My heart hurts for you."

Yes… there was a verse of Scripture shared that was meaningful to him.

Yes… there was prayer that followed for Marshall.

Yes… there was a final sincere question of "What can I do for you?"

But five words - "my heart hurts for you" - reminded me I was not alone. Like the One who said "I will never leave you nor forsake you." **(Hebrews 15:5)**.

Marshall was in NICU for 17 days. He's now a good pitcher and a scrappy catcher for his high school baseball team.

It was 15 years ago I felt sweet kindness in action. It has marked me for life. The Bishop was like God with skin.

"Gracious words are like a honeycomb, sweetness to the soul and health to the body." **(Proverbs 16:24)**.

"Thank you for sharing. This is so difficult. My heart hurts for you."

Sweet honey.

Just like something Jesus would say.

# Everydayness

The problem with life? It's so daily.

What I am discovering in my faith journey: everydayness bugs me.

It's easier to think of what I would do in a war, or show faith thru a hurricane than figure out how to live each day without grumbling.

It's in the small moments of frustration (anger) along with life's interruptions that make me stir crazy.

"Do all things without grumbling or disputing" I read in **Philippians 2:14**. ALL things? Sure.

My theology rises up with the War in Ukraine, but my daily grind finds me riddled with low grade anxiety.

I know better. But to tell myself to cheer up doesn't work.

The issue: I think God is too busy to touch my typical day. My practical theology really consists of ignoring God in the routine.

I pay attention to God in crisis. But to welcome God into a maddening committee meeting is beneath His pay grade.

I lose my composure in the midst of my irritating maintenance... which is the vast majority of the Christian life.

When I lose the car keys my smooth facade of control is disrupted. That's when I am exposed.

As CS Lewis says, "I am merely amusing myself when I ask for patience in persecution as I grumble about every inconvenience."

What's the solution when the roof leaks, the car breaks down, the kitchen sink clogs?

I must give up my right of control. To kill the belief that in my average day I have the right to be annoyed.

It's slaying the false belief that God is only interested in the Really. Big. Things. That in lousy sleep or a house wrecked by kids – I'm on my own.

The truth is I am never on my own. The same God who counts the hair on our heads is the One who died and rose again.

I see how tightly I cling to control and how little control I actually have. Out of control, I feel stuck and suppress the truth.

I brood. I mutter. I withdraw. I throw Spiritual Tantrums.

And when it's over, I put on my veil again. But Jesus is always there to meet me, saying give it to Me.

Both in catastrophes and backed up sinks.

# Happiness

For years, I have said "Never make a decision in a mood. Think about it today, decide tomorrow."

At times I add a pithy PS: "Feelings are real, just not reliable."

All of that has a colonel of truth. But my tendency is to throw the proverbial baby out with the bath.

I think feelings get a bad rap.

I have been told all my Christian life that joy is not happiness. I then hear a definition of joy that sounds sterile, mechanical and joy-less.

Something like joy is a "quiet controlled confidence in the sovereignty of God." Yawn.

Match that with King David dancing half naked before the Lord in celebration. Match that with the 98 times in the Bible that God is delighted. Or over 400 times He's glad.

I am working now in Krakow Poland. One of the reasons I travel is it makes me happy.

Last night I heard an hour long concert by a world renowned pianist who played 11 arrangements by Chopin. It was awesome.

Music makes me happy. Exquisite harmony stirs melody in my heart. **(Ephesians 5:19)**.

I think the Holy Spirit sings in sync, bubbling up His unique brand of happiness.

Here's my question: Do you think God is Happy?

I believe He's immeasurably happy. The happiest in the Universe. And we are created in His Image.

Echoes of His joy are everywhere: in nature, in a kid's wide-eyed innocence, in a country like Poland that embraces Ukrainians as "guests" – not refugees.

The jubulant scene in The Chosen makes John 2 and Christ's first miracle spell binding.

If you don't smile at Jesus dancing and laughing in that scene, you're dead– you just haven't been buried yet.

Yes, the world is a mess. Yes, God is in charge of it. Yes, lots of things don't make sense.

So I have a choice. I can wallow in the whys... or I can revel in the rejoicing.

It's true: happiness IS a choice. And I'm not just being Pollyanna.

When our daughter Mindy gets upset, which is seldom, her husband John David says, "But Mindy... you're beautiful and you're going to heaven."

She is and she will.

There is a big difference between forced giddiness and Spirit inspired happiness. If you ask me, consistent joy is the greatest proof we walk with Jesus.

In the end, I have joy because God says to His followers...

"You're Beautiful and you're going to heaven."

# Easter

Soon after I became a Christian, I struggled with doubts.

I asked a guy named Charles Ryrie, "How do you really become a Christian?"

He paused and said, "It means saying yes to a promise."

And what was that promise?

Jesus: "If you believe in Me you have eternal life." ***(John 6: 47)***.

So clear. But most of us doubt it's that simple. I did.

Surely I have to do something more than that! Stop the things I habitually do. The words I say about others. The carousing. The _____.

"You mean to tell me that someone could live a selfish, evil life and then simply say yes to Jesus on his death bed and go to heaven?!"

No, I'm not saying that. The Bible does. ***(John 3:16)***.

Our underlying assumption: we must add something to grace to get to heaven. No free lunch, right? Wrong. ***(Ephesians 2: 8-9)***.

The hardest part about grasping grace is swallowing our pride and saying, "I don't deserve heaven any more than Judas, Hitler, Stalin, Putin or the worst criminal."

Sorry to those whose names I just listed. I have no idea where they will spend eternity. If I think I know because of their behavior, I've missed grace altogether.

I go to heaven because of my belief, not my behavior.

Salvation is inexpressibly expensive for God. But... there is nothing I can do to pay for it. Earn it. Add to it.

The thief on the Cross asked Jesus to save him. And the famous words that Jesus rsponded in agony, "Today you will be with me in paradise." ***(Luke 23: 42—43)***.

The thief would never make restitution, attend church, sing a hymn, take communion, or make a donation. He had nothing to offer Christ, no way to pay Him back.

Neither do we.

Randy Alcorn writes, " Imagine there is a King who invites you to live with him, even though you murdered his son. Suppose you saved your money, brought it to the King and said, "Here... I'm paying you back."

Imagine how the King would respond? He would be rightly insulted. It cheapen's his son's death.

There is one thing God cannot do. He cannot lie. He keeps His promises. He guarantees eternal life for all who believe.

My dad believed Christ's promise on his death bed. My brother who died of a heroin OD did.

Nothing in my hands I bring. Simply to the Cross I cling.

He is not here. He is Risen!

Simply believe it.

# Wait For It

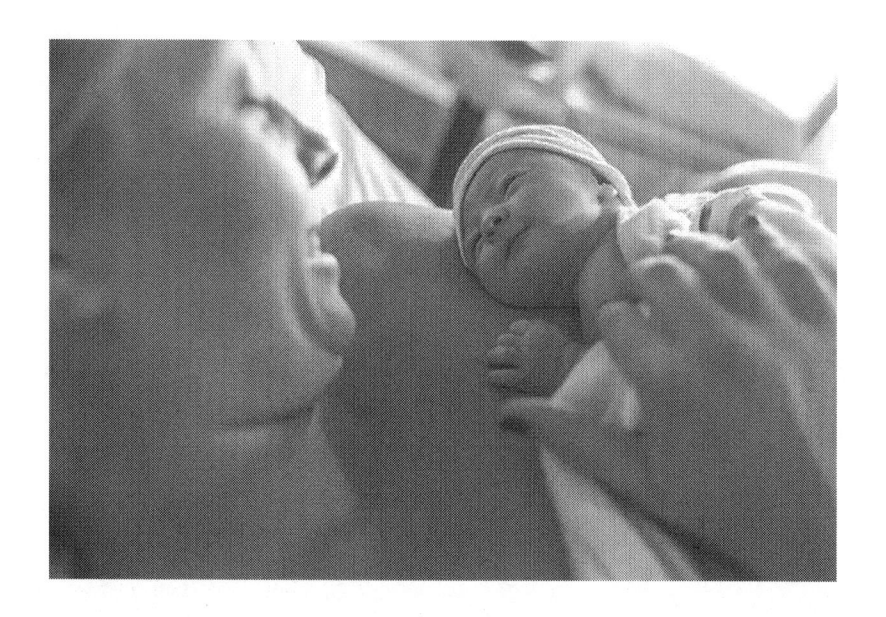

I turned 76 over the weekend.

It's the oddest thing. When I speak these days I sometimes mention my age.

I expect the audience to gasp and say "No way!"

They don't.

I have noticed that my doctor looks like he just reached puberty.

What's my biggest take away after living three quarters of a century?

I made two lists on my birthday... the worst things that have happened to me... and the best.

I discovered something interesting.

Most of my best things came out of my worst things.

Just like the Easter message, life really does come out of death.

My deepest happiness, to my surprise, came out of my strongest disappointments.

Jesus said it best. For Believers, our sorrows will be turned into joy. He gave an illustration of a mother giving birth.

What caused the pain–the baby–also causes the joy. **(John 16:20)** The baby doesn't just replace the pain, but transforms it.

Joseph said of his trials "You meant evil against me, But God meant it for good."

He doesn't say God made the best out of bad circumstances. He was pouring out His love all along.

Doesn't Easter prove one thing? He's earned the right to be trusted.

As childlike as it sounds, I have learned to trust God when things don't YET make sense.

C.S. Lewis wrote to a Christian in America who thought she was dying.

"Can you not see death as a friend and deliverer? Has the world been so kind to you that you regret leaving it? Our Lord says, 'Peace child. Relax and let go. I will catch you.'"

He adds, "Of course this may not be the end. Then make it a good rehearsal."

One second after I go to heaven I'll understand. So will you.

Keep rehearsing.

It's worth the wait.

# Longing for Home

As I grew up, I listened to Paul Harvey, the iconic storyteller.

He would conclude his riveting stories with, "Now you know the rest of the story."

I have discovered God loves cliffhangers and nail-biters. He is the God of surprise endings.

He has another haymaker in the works. A really big one.

When Christians gather on that Last Day, trillions of plot points will come together, and millions with cry out like the voice of many waters… singing…

"THAT was the greatest story we've ever heard!"

**Romans 8:28** will come true.

Faith is like a forward memory. It allows us to believe a promise has already happened.

In heaven, we'll work backward and turn even the worst agony into good.

When Aslan dies in Narnia, He explains to the witch that death itself starts working backward. The curse is reversed.

It's why the worst day in history is called Good Friday. Because Sunday's coming.

CS Lewis explains, "There have been times when I think we do not desire heaven but more often I wonder whether we have desired anything else."

One of my favorite characters in The Chronicles of Narnia is the brave mouse Reepicheep.

He longed for Aslan's country, but longed far more for the King of that country.

The courageous mouse says, "I will sail East on the Dawn Treader. When she fails me, I shall paddle in my coracle. When she sinks, I shall swim with my four paws. When I can swim no longer, I shall sink with my nose to the sunrise."

His deepest longing for heaven. I find myself increasingly there.

This world never keeps its promises. It's simply not our Sunrise.

Could it be we were made for another world?

Yes we are!

The Bible says "We wait eagerly on tiptoes for the revealing of the sons of God." **(Romans 8:19)**.

Every day I am more like Reepicheep on tiptoes. My nose to the Sunrise.

Longing for Home.

# Farming

I recently wondered: What if God was Great and He was a Grouch?

After all, our entire theology is built on one belief: God is Good.

To our relief, the God of the Bible does not whine, pout or complain. He instead delights in everything He does.

Because all things we experience pass through His Hand, He always steps back and says, "That's good. Really good."

God is like a farmer who might end the day with a field all torn up from plowing. He's just fine with the mess.

Why? Because He's not done with the field. He enjoys the plowing in anticipation of a bumper crop.

What seems messy turns happy. So it is with us.

I'm pondering this truth: We can be happy because God is Happy with Himself.

He's content with half finished projects, unhealthy bodies, and a groaning universe because of glorious outcomes. He knows how the Story ends.

He's the Author of it.

It gives me great comfort to think God never shrugs and says, "I could have done better."

Here's my take on God's sovereignty and our free will in a nutshell: Do the best you can; then relax... the future is fixed.

We are to walk in good works SET before us. He sets. We walk.

To think I can thwart the will of God is like a bug hitting my windshield going 80.

No, God will not interfere with my free will. I can jump of a skyscraper, enjoy the first part of the trip... but land with a thud and I will not like it.

He doesn't delight in all we do, just like He wasn't pleased when Adam plucked Eden's fruit and plunged us into a huge mess.

But He redeems, restores and rescues. And reverses even my rebellion when He turns on His Divine Mixmaster.

Tragedy to triumph is His specialty. There's one short verse that sums it all up: He is pleased by all He does **(Psalm 115:9)**.

Two phrases I lean on in my wilderness wondering: "But God..." and "Not YET!"

For the unbeliever, this life is the best it gets. For the Christ Follower... this life is the worst it gets.

The harvest is ahead. So take heart fellow farmers. Keep plowing.

# Shhhh!

Quiet is way underrated.

There is no greater beauty than words aptly spoken. **(Proverbs 25:11)**.

Except maybe when verbal turmoil is met with eloquent silence.

We Christians are quick to say "The Lord fights our battles."

Then proceed to don the armor and deliver a knock out punch.

The untamable tongue. **(James 3:8)**.

I have never been criticized for staying quiet. I have invariably walked back the best argument I've ever regretted.

Forgive me if I have a private talk with myself this morning. It's not pretty, but you can listen in.

Randy, when you think you know better, keep your mouth shut. Maybe listen to understand.

Stay quiet. When you have a clever, stinging retort, stay quiet.

Nobody can deliver a better crafted insult than me. I never had to go to school to learn how to be cutting.

Acerbic whit, cascading words unchecked remind me of the truth: where there are many words, sin is unavoidable. **(Proverbs 10:19)**.

I realize the topic of reckless words- gossip, sarcasm, lies, half truths- is a struggle for all of us.

Here's my salty cure....maybe yours too. I need to shut my mouth and stay quiet, stay quiet, stay quiet.

Embrace the "I don't knows", the awkward silence, the urge to dispute. Avoid my misplaced "brilliance".

Without sounding overly religious, I need to wait for the Holy Spirit to prompt me.

I realize that sounds airy fairy. Here's how I know if's from God.

By staying quiet... my delayed words have a chance to be edifying. Gentle. Even thoughtful.

Reaction can become a response. Unwholesome can become wholesome. Rancor can become kind.

Words are like water: they can quench thirst or warm the bath. They can also flood the river and destroy.

"A fool vents all his feelings, but the wise man holds them back." **(Proverbs 29:11)**. Ouch.

"Do you see a man hasty in his words? There is more hope for a fool than for him." **(Proverbs 29: 20)** Ugh.

It's like God has a Divine Finger to His all knowing Lips.

Whispering to me, "Shhhh! I opened the Tomb. I can open your mouth."

# Feet of Clay

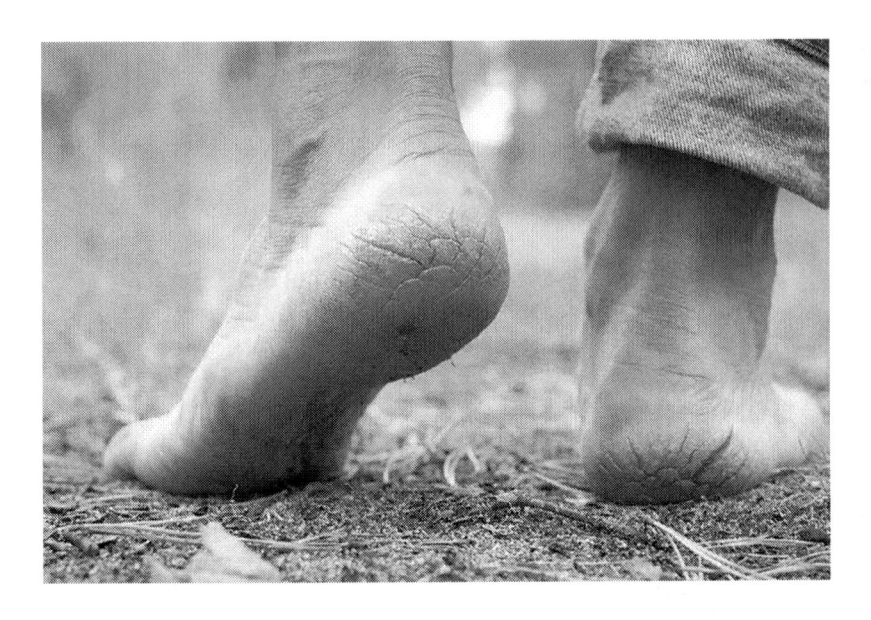

As I grow older, I notice that I am fulfilling Biblical prophecy: The outer man decays.

No geezer needs a Bible to prove that.

One of the first things to go literally South were my feet.

Somewhere between pesky callouses, cracked toe nails and heels that could sandpaper a wall, it got downright ugly.

I take no small comfort that the Bible places our feet on higher ground.

I remember the first time a group of Believers read from John 13 about Jesus washing the disciples dirty feet.

And how shocked I was when the leader washed my feet and how I in turn washed his.

It was emotional, humbling, memorable.

One of my favorite women in the Bible is Mary of Bethany. She's of Mary and Martha fame, sisters who also had a brother named Lazarus.

At first , we find Mary curled up at Jesus feet. Our Lord says "She has chosen the ONE thing necessary." To know Him.

Then we see her falling at the Master's feet. Questioning Jesus' timing with Lazarus who's been dead four days. Now she's hurt and confused.

Finally she worships the Savior, lavishing perfume on His feet, wiping them with her hair. Now she adores Him.

I think it's a beautiful threefold picture of the Christian life: We learn, we question, we worship.

Then we repeat the cycle until heaven.

I remember when I first became a Christian, I couldn't get enough of His words. What a life of peace.

Then came the weaning times, tested by heartache and trials. What's going on here?

Then seasons of both...His blessed ways and His testing ways. Will I still worship Him? Where else can I go?

Our human feet may have creepy toe fungus. Brittle nails. Embarrassing discolor. Bent by age.

Kinda like our messy lives. Feet of clay.

But our spiritual feet, as it says in **Ephesians 6:15**, are able to deliver a Gospel of Peace.

So much so that God says, "How beautiful are the feet of him who brings good news of salvation." **(Isaiah 52:7)**.

My Divine Podiatrist says my feet are beautiful.

Who knew?

Helps me stand firm.

# Tim

**TIMOTHY KELLER**
**1950-2023**

I have never been more nervous.

As I have traveled to mission fields, I've met Kings of African countries. Dined with heads of State. Spoken to a Parliament.

But as I stood in a line to shake his hand, I was gripped with an irregular heartbeat, found myself almost hyperventilating.

I prayed my butterflies would fly in formation.

I kept telling myself he's just a man. Puts his pants on one leg at a time. Just breathe. It wasn't working.

This was my hero, my inspiration, my mentor from afar.

I was getting ready to meet Tim Keller.

Last Friday was a great day for Tim. He went Home to Heaven. What a coronation celebration he must have had!

After all, he was the one who said, "The worst thing that can happen to you is also the best thing that can happen to you."

In no more pain after three years battling pancreatic cancer. Tim has crossed the Veil.

Embraced by His Savior, he now sees in full, set free, dancing with joy inexpressible. Permanently healed.

He was our brilliant CS Lewis. Our encouraging Barnabas. Our humble Mary.

He was like Jesus to me.

And yet Tim would take his place at the lowest seat, reminding us he wasn't.

We could talk about his books... 3 million sold. We could talk about his messages, riveting and wise. Maybe discuss his New York City Church, started from scratch, now 5,000 seekers.

But to me, what separated Tim from all the rest was how he shared the Gospel. I have literally listened to hundreds of his messages.

And every time he talked about the Resurrection I wept with joy. His grace-saturated Easter message meant everything to Tim. And also to a wide eyed student like me.

For the day I met Tim Keller, I prepared a short message. I rehearsed it standing in line. I was going to tell him how he changed my life.

Truth is, I couldn't say a word. I just shook his hand and stared at him, tears welling up.

He gently smiled as I swallowed hard. Somehow he knew. Prophets are like that.

One of the first things I want to do when I get to heaven is to tell him, "You are my joy and my crown." **(Philippians 4:1)**.

In his last words, he thanked his family, expressed his gratitude to God for his time on earth and said, "I cannot wait to see Jesus. Send me Home."

He has now been summoned.

Welcome Home Tim.

# Delight

Have you ever wondered how God puts up with us?

You know. A roll of His divine eyes. A slap on His divine forehead. We are such knuckleheads.

Did you know there's a place the Bible where He regrets creating us? **(Genesis 6:6)**.

Right before we had rain for the first time. Lots of it.

He's promised to love us. He can't help Himself. God IS love.

But here's my question? Do you think God LIKES us? I think love and like are two very different things.

I mean let's be honest. There are some people I can't stand. Some of those are Christians. I have verses on loving them, but liking them? Fat chance.

And it goes both ways. I feel like saying, "The Jesus in me loves the Jesus in you... but that's about as far as it goes."

If I like someone it means I delight in being with them. I enjoy them.

The commandment to love involves sacrifice, obligation, obedience. OK... I get that. Even my enemies.

But here's the question for me: Does God really like us?

More often than not, with God knowing my most intimate ways, there's no way I think He likes me.

In Kelly Kapic's excellent book, "You're Only Human" he says: "Forgetting God's delight and joy in us stunts our ability to enjoy God's love."

Could it be He chases me down because He delights in me? He actually enjoys me? I think He does.

How could a holy and perfect God LIKE a sinful, weak and wayward me? I've had my deepest doubts.

But, If true, it touches heartstrings I didn't know I had. It makes me thick in the throat.

"The Lord your God is with you, the Mighty Warrior who saves. He takes great delight in you...and rejoices over you with singing." *(Zephaniah 3:17)*.

How about that? He saves me AND delights in me. Likes me so much he sings over me with joy.

He created my quirks, weirdness, bents and calls them good.

He knows I am made from dust. He knows how hard it is to be us.

And still loves me. Amazingly, He even likes me.

And you too.

# Small Fries

I often show more grace to McDonalds than I do my church.

Today it seems like there's a 50/50 chance of getting my food order wrong. A wrong drink, no ketchup, cold fries. But I keep coming back.

One guy put it this way, "McDonalds can mess up your order 101 times, and you'll keep going back. One thing goes wrong at church and you quit?"

I go to a great church: 115 programs meeting needs, 250 staff, two excellent teaching pastors.

Yet from what I hear, our staff is bombarded by unsigned emails, angered by a pastor's message, loud music, not enough hymns sung, cold coffee. Ad nauseam.

And so the disgruntled take their business elsewhere. Then elsewhere. Then elsewhere again.

I think we're producing a generation of church tramps and sermon sifters. Meet my "needs" or I leave.

Have we become so thin skinned? I think we have.

Too many of us think we're passengers on cruise ships, not battle ships. Consumers not warriors.

The Apostle Paul refereed church fights and personal grievances constantly.

Christians are always stepping on each other's toes. Given enough time, people will hurt your feelings.

One of my favorite counselors said "Ministry in the church is like jumping into a sewer with a can of deodorant and it doesn't work."

Paul admonishes, "Put on compassion, kindness, humility, gentleness and patience. Bear with one another. Forgive one another if anyone has a grievance against you." ***(Colossians 3: 12-13)***.

And then he adds a P.S., "Just as the Lord has forgiven you, also forgive others."

Getting our angelic feathers ruffled is more certain in church than McDonalds getting our order wrong.

I remember one person who continually got to me. Pushed all my buttons.

I thought I had forgiven him until, as I was taking communion one Sunday, he walked into the sanctuary. I bit down and cracked my plastic communion cup. Oops.

What has helped me? When I remember how much the Lord has forgiven me.

When I do... their offense seems like small fries.

# A KonMari Heart

Her book zoomed to number one on the New York Times bestseller list.

It coined a new word for our English dictionaries: KonMari. A guide to getting organized.

Marie Kondo, author of "The Life - changing Magic of Tidying up" gave us the anti hoarding litmus test.

Does your possession still "spark joy in you?"

If it does, keep it; if not, throw it out. So, KonMari your life. Happiness awaits.

When we had a fire that destroyed our home 9 years ago, we KonMaried a bunch of stuff.

High school memorabilia, old shirts and shoes.

But recently I read where a woman decluttered her husband.

Once she disposed of her non-sparking possessions,

and still lacked happiness, she got rid of her non-sparking hubby.

I had to wonder what was next? Siblings, friends, coworkers, pastors?

You're KonMaried! Adios amigo.

How about vocations, people, churches, etc.

We say things like "I just don't feel happy anymore. I feel my heart is leading me in another direction."

Scripture has something to say about it: "The heart is deceitful and wicked above all things. Who can know it?" **(Jeremiah 17:9)**.

As one guy said it well, "We elect as our leader the least trustworthy, most self serving, most terrible guide imaginable: our own heart."

The predictable result: "There's a way that seems right to man, but the end thereof is death." **(Proverbs 14:12)**.

While feelings are one voice in a jury of our peers, emotions cannot be the jury foreman.

When my decisions are based solely on my satisfaction, my contentment, and my fulfillment the word Narcissism is our guide. Perseverance?

Oh, please.

My point? Do not trust your heart; inform it. That's where the Word of God comes in.

When storm clouds come and your plane feels like it's flying upside down, trust the instrument panel.

Far too often, following our heart really means running from God.

And racing to the idol of Me.

KonMari it.

# Encouragement

I've noticed when people say, "With all due respect" they soon clearly don't.

Could it be that criticism springs from an assumption of superior intelligence?

I'm going to go out on a limb: there is no such thing as "constructive criticism." People say they want it, but they don't.

"I am only trying to help," they say. In reality, their words make you feel small.

Criticism is destructive. Encouragement is constructive.

I have a pastor friend who is an encourager. He planted a church in a rough part of town. He has a growing congregation filled with broken down homeless, struggling prostitutes, cast off druggies.

They come empty handed, starved for a sustaining word. They know they are sinners saved by grace.

My friend encourages them with wonderful stories of God's rescue and redemption in Jesus, with a gleeful belly laugh and a heavy dose of hope.

I'll tell you what he does: he restores their dignity.

He actually believes they too are made in the Image of God. Imagine that.

The Scripture says, "Encourage one another daily so that you will not be hardened by the deceitfulness of sin." **(Hebrews 3:13)**.

Encouragement softens us to hear the truth. Criticism hardens us, makes us defensive, stirs up resentment.

A Welsh Monk named Geoffrey of Monmouth published a book in 1136 about the history of the British Kings.

He wrote it to encourage a downcast band of Brits. He wanted them to see themselves as part of a magnificent and proud heritage.

He wrote of Merlyn, Guinevere, Arthur and the Knights of the Round Table. Not ONE word of it was true. At least not yet.

Geoffrey saw something in his people they did not see in themselves. That's what encouragement does.

The most important people in your life are the ones who believe in you more than you believe in yourself.

Look back at Hebrews 3:13... It says encourage one another daily... "while it is called today." What does that mean?

One day we will no longer need encouragement. Time will cease. No more todays. We will be with the Great Encourager.

But for now, while your life lasts, do it daily. You might turn a discouraged Lancelot into a King Arthur.

# Time and Eternity

Whenever I speak now, I ask one question. "How much do you think about eternity?"

I am always surprised by the blank stares I get. Dead silence gives me a clue: not very much.

Lest you think I am an old geezer and close to crossing the Veil (which is undeniable), I ask the question to my age group as well.

Same response: Like I was an alien from Mars speaking gibberish.

So... how much do YOU think about eternity?

I may be mentally deranged, but I think about it hours a day. Not like a monk eating birdseed on a Tibet mountaintop.

But at some level, eternity dogs my steps. I am obsessed by the life to come.

I believe you cannot be earthly good unless you're heavenly minded.

Here's my thinking: Rarity always determines value. And the reverse is true... commonality decreases value.

Ben Franklin is right, "Time is the stuff life is made of". So... are our lives common or rare?

My Father in Law is 103.5 years of age. Rare? Yes. But compared to eternity, a blip on the screen.

I think we've been duped. We look at the second hand on our clocks and watch it go round and round. All the time in the world.

I don't think a watch is the best indicator of time. Instead, maybe flip over an hour glass every morning.

I'll be the first to admit I don't understand time. Is there time in heaven? I don't know. Probably not.

And time management? A myth. I cannot turn 5 minutes into 7. I only manage activities in time, not time itself.

In comparison to my life on earth, eternity is looooong. So my days, and yours, are rare and priceless. How rare?

Like a vapor, like sparks flying upward, like a flower that fades. **(James 4:14, Job 5:6-7, Psalm 103:15)**.

God will not be asking about our shell collection when we chat in eternity. He WILL ask about how we discharged the talents he gave us. *(Matthew 25)*.

Life's opportunities are rolling by on wheels. Redeem them.

One suggestion: since God is the divine matchmaker of abilities and opportunities - let's start by reading our Bible.

Check out Romans 12. Maybe start there.

As you read, ask God to stir your mind, spark your heart, and do something about it.

If we don't, one year from now we'll be one year older. And no wiser *(Psalm 90:12)*.

Three practical things tell me how much I think about eternity. My calendar, my checkbook...

And an hour glass.

# Adored

I say the word adored a lot lately. I know it's not very manly.

More than any time in my life... I find myself adoring children, especially our 12 grandkids.

Am I getting sappy in my old age? I sure hope so. It's about time.

I find myself watching adoring parents as they talk to their kids.

Here's what I have noticed. When a kid feels a look of 'one and only" from a mom or dad they come alive. Makes me feel alive too.

It melts me as few other things do these days. Mesmerizing, almost hypnotic.

I have never met a kid who was adored who was insecure. No striving, no craving attention.

It is beautiful.

I think Jesus longs to be adored too. He is beautiful.

When I find myself adoring Him, I don't wonder if I'm doing enough.

I don't fret, wondering if my "being and doing" is off center.

His company is enough. HE is enough. The more I spend time with Jesus... I find Him a companion, a friend, a comfort, a delight.

His beauty prompts my duty. His tenderness spurs my tasks.

I find myself working less, worshipping more. The irony is it gets done quicker - and better.

I think He wants my company more than my calling.

I am an ice cream freak. Never met a flavor I didn't like. But if you asked me to describe butter pecan ice cream,

I'd just mumble.

I might suggest you just taste it. As in, "Taste the Lord for He is Good." **(Psalm 34:8)**.

Adoration is like that - hard to define. But we know it when we taste it. Its like being lost in wonder.

It's Mary at His feet. It's being still and knowing He's God. It's the key to prayer.

Reverence and fear go along with blissful adoration. Our ability to adore goes to the heart of who we really are.

It's wonderful when an earthly father adores his kids.

It's indescribable when our Heavenly Father adores us. ***(Zephaniah 3:17)***.

I get spiritually sappy.

# Lord of the Feast

What if instead of working harder at being a good Christian, we simply enjoyed Jesus more?

Commands like be glad, exude joy and savor the abundant life sound a lot more fun.

And if there's anybody who should be having fun, it's Christians. We know how the Story ends.

Take your faith seriously, but not yourself. I feel like the guy who said if joy is in your heart, please inform your face.

Faces that look like they've been weaned on a dill pickle are not exactly calling cards for Jesus.

There's a passage in Luke 10 where the disciples are given a serious commission: go cast out demons and heal the sick.

They come back like little kids, giddy at "Watching Satan falling like lightning."

But Jesus says, "Nevertheless, do not rejoice in this. Rather that your names are written in the Book of Life."

What's fascinating is the word "rejoice" used means to run and skip with hilarity. Like a child. Why?

Because the war is over. Yes, the battles are ahead, but you've already won. Your names are written in indelible ink.

Since I crunched my hip a year ago I haven't run nor skipped with hilarity. And I've missed it. But my skipping body awaits.

Rejoice, again I say Rejoice! **(Philippians 4:4)** A command so important Paul says it twice.

When C.S Lewis said , "Joy is the serious business of heaven", he nailed it.

I no longer think there's a difference between happiness and joy.

When I have a great belly laugh I don't wonder any more if its from my circumstances or from my Lord.

Frankly, I'm too old to debate it. Exhausting religion died at the Cross.

I just let the endorphins flow, thanking God I have nothing to prove, nothing to lose.

The Lord of the Feast now ferments my wine and bids me to taste His goodness.

Who am I to disagree?

Let's have some fun.

See you at the Party.

# Givers and Takers

It's scorching hot in Texas.

Lawns are choking and air conditioners are struggling to keep up.

A July day in Dallas always reminds me of a November day in Israel.

It was while there I learned about two seas in the land where Jesus walked.

One is the Sea of Galilee and the other the Sea of Death. We call it the Dead Sea because nothing grows there: no fish, no vegetation.

The Sea of Galilee is full of life and power... So I asked the obvious. Why is one dead and the other alive?

Our guide told us that both Seas receive water from the Jordan River, where I was baptized.

"But" he said, 'the Dead Sea has only one opening. It gets water from the Jordan but has no outlet. The Galilee receives water but it has an outlet. It gives out what it receives."

It gives out what it receives.

I have found that undrinkable people are always receiving and seldom giving.

To press the analogy: A life that gives back what it receives is fresh and alive. Other lives give off an aroma of death. **(II Corinthians 2:16)**.

Two kinds of people: Givers and Takers.

I like how one person put it, "Blessed are those who can give without remembering and take without forgetting."

Jesus said it this way, "I would rather you be hot or cold water. If you are lukewarm I will spit you out of my mouth." **(Revelation 3: 15-16)**.

Cold water is good for quenching thirst. Hot water is good for bathing. Lukewarm water is good for neither.

The Dead Sea is literally lukewarm in temperature; tepid to the core.

What you do with what you have been given is what counts. If you live for yourself, that's exactly who you end up with.

"It's more blessed to give than receive." **(Acts 20:35)** Could Jesus be right? Every time.

It'll be 106 F. in Dallas today.

Lukewarm water just won't satisfy.

# A Person and a Place

Ever had an itch you couldn't scratch?

When I was in Acapulco on our honeymoon, I stayed out in the sun way too long.

Even pure aloe vera was useless. I went crazy with itching.

And the more I tried to calm the misery, the more my scratching turned hellish, craving for relief.

Nothing would satisfy.

My longing for heaven is sorta like that. I am really Homesick. And no matter what I do to sooth my aching for Home,

I still itch.

A new job, a long awaited vacation, a new car, a cabin in the woods, a duplex in Hawaii may sooth the itch for awhile... then it comes roaring back.

As Randy Alcorn puts it, "What we really want is the Person we were made for and the Place we were made for."

Jesus is that Person and Heaven is that Place.

You may have the same problem I have... always feeling like I'm missing something? I am.

I have misdiagnosed my illness. It's really a case of homesickness.

What if I worked harder, drank more, slept longer, got married, went to counseling... then the craving will end.

Wrong. It won't.

Nothing but a Person and a Place will fully satisfy. We are searching for something we can't find on earth.

Here's the amazing thing: God made us that way.

He made us hungry for something else. We have an insatiable restlessness that can only be erased in Jesus Christ and the Life to come.

He alone can tame the untamable. Sooth the flammable.

Here's the surprise: Yearning for it is very healthy. This longing is like a compass. It can point us to The True North.

But like a fire escaping the fire place, it can burn us in a thousand ways. We are experts at corrupting a good thing.

The cure for homesickness is not wanting more and more. It's pursuing what the Bible calls The Unseen Things. **(Hebrews 11:3)**.

It happens when I look beyond the majesty of creation, the laugh of a child, the taste of savory food and I see a Person and a Place.

Call it the echo of heaven. A preview of coming attractions. The Bible says it's like seeing through a dark glass.

Yes, our homesickness has been misdiagnosed. Want the cure for your relentless itch?

Trade the Aloe Vera for the Alpha Omega.

# Appointments

I tend to be late for appointments. There's really no excuse.

I either lose track of time or get engrossed in some discussion.

It's amazing how often the Bible talks about appointments. Over 500 times. But not the ones I make. The ones God makes.

And He's never late.

I was reading the Book of Jonah recently and I kept noticing that the reluctant prophet kept running into divine appointments.

With a large fish, a leafy plant, and a worm.

Got swallowed by one, found comfort in one and was annoyed by one. The Bible says all of them were appointed.

Here's what's fascinating: "Only after them was Jonah able to know the heart of God."

I want to know the heart of God.

Today is July 24, 2023. I know I'll have appointments today orchestrated by God. Most will seem like unplanned interruptions.

And that's where I'll find God's Heart.

In August of 1965 I was headed to Kansas State University to play baseball. Overnight, God interrupted that plan and made me a Razorback.

That appointment changed everything. Two years later I found God's heart as I became a Christian. Or rather He found me.

What we call coincidences God calls appointments. As Proverbs 20:24 says," The Lord directs our steps. So how can anyone understand their own way?" We can't. **(Romans 11:33)**.

His appointments are a mystery, wrapped in a puzzle, sealed with an enigma. Past finding out.

As the Yiddish proverb says, "We plan, God laughs."

Our job is to do the best we can, wherever we are, with what we have. He keeps the appointment book.

There's an appointed time for everything under the sun. **(Ecclesiastes 3)**. That includes meeting God now **(John 3:16)** and meeting Him later **(Hebrews 9:27)**.

The first appointment is voluntary, the second mandatory.

It is appointed that man should die once and then the judgment.

It's already scheduled.

None of us will miss it.

And He won't be late.

# Riches

I read this morning that Jeff Bezos of Amazon fame has a net worth of $154 Billion.

He rents a home on a cozy beach front in Southern California for $600,000 a month... 7.2 million a year.

That is not a typo. Six hundred thousand a month. All for 5,500 square feet. BTW, it's unfurnished.

Almost $1K an hour.

Rents it from musician Kenny G.

I think G stands for Gotcha.

It has beach front property, a pool and a small guest house.

It blows all of my categories.

You know what my first thought was? He'd better hope the Big One doesn't quake him into the Pacific Ocean...

...swallowing his rental bungalow AND his $500 million yacht.

After I read about his mind boggling finances, I walked downstairs and noticed a quote on the wall behind our $25 coffee maker...

"Never let your happiness be based on something you can lose." C.S. Lewis of Oxford.

And then an immediate afterthought: "I will never leave you nor forsake you." Jesus of Nazareth.

Give me Jesus.

Along with the priceless home He's building for those who believe. *(John 14:3)*.

Rent's free.

The view is stunning.

And our Architect designed the Universe.

# Two Lions

There was a desperate unemployed man who took an unusual job to support his family.

He worked at a local zoo: dressing up in a ape costume to entertain the crowd.

His job was to fly over the Lion's den on a rope and tease the prowling lions.

One day, as the crowd watched in awe, he slipped and fell into the the Lion's den. He panicked.

Forgetting he was not a chimp, he began to yell "Help! Save me!"

A Lion began to slowly stalk him. Knowing he was a goner the counterfeit ape yelled louder for help.

The King of the Jungle slowly crept up to the trembling Ape and whispered, "Shut up stupid or we'll both lose our jobs."

I've told that story from Ukraine to China and it never fails to get a response.

I read a story yesterday about a zoo in Eastern China accused of using men dressing up as bears. They are denying it.

Of course, it's the same zoo that was fined last year for painting donkeys and calling them zebras.

We live in a time where it's hard to believe anything you see or read. From photoshopping to AI.

But there is one counterfeiter you can always count on being deceptive: he's called the father of lies, one who masquerades as the angel of light. *(John 8:44).*

This one is real. He loves the comic image of horns and a pitchfork.

Fun stuff until he kills and destroys a ministry, a family, a church. Interestingly, he not only kills but also destroys. As if death wasn't enough for him.

We fight as Believers three battle fronts: The world system, our own flesh and the Devil from Hell. *(James 3:15).*

Satan is alive and thinks he's well. He's not. Defeated at the Cross, he's still on the prowl. Literally.
As a lion who seeks to devour. *(I Peter 5:8).*

Only this defanged lion wants us to lose more than our jobs.

Derailing our ministries, tempting our weakness, inflaming our addictions - he stalks .

But unlike the costumed chimp who cries out, "Help! Save me!"...

We have a Roaring Lion who does. *(Hosea 11:10).*

# Goats

My favorite cartoon growing up was Tom and Jerry. Closely followed by Mickey Mouse and Pluto.

I've always loved animal duos.

But I've never heard of a unique pairing until this weekend: a goat and a racehorse.

These two are not only paired up at races like the Kentucky Derby but they become friends. Barn Buddies.

Why? The goat has an amazing calming effect on a jittery horse before a big race. Who knew?

High strung horses who lose their appetites, run around in their stalls, gasping for air suddenly become calm with a goat.

It got me thinking. Am I like a goat or more like a racehorse to others? Do I bring peace or anxiety?

About six months ago I read that QB Tom Brady was a GOAT. When I was growing up, a goat was the one who lost the game.

But not now: Greatest. Of. All. Time.

As weird as this sounds, I want to be a goat- who brings shalom.

I'm encouraged deeply when my daughters "just want to hear dad's voice" during trying times.

When I become a nervous nellie I long to hear another voice: "In Me you have peace." **(John 16: 33)**.

I think what we want most in life is peace. His peace. No chance to be "at peace with all men" without it. **(Romans 12:18)**.

I never thought I would say I want Jesus to be my GOAT. To reverently ask Him to be my Barn Buddy.

The Bible urges this old horse to finish the race **(2 Timothy 4:7)**. Run with endurance **(Hebrews 12:1)**. Receive the Prize **(I Cor. 9:27)**.

But best of all?

The Greatest of All Time meets me at the finish line.

# The Silence of God

When the Japanese invaded New Guinea during WWII, Russell and Darlene Rose were serving as missionaries.

They were arrested and separated.

Russell's last words to his wife were "Remember one thing, dear. God said that He would never leave us nor forsake us."

She never saw him again.

The women were taken to a prison camp where she suffered from dysentery, malaria and beriberi. Much in solitary confinement.

She found out later her husband had died in 1944.

Throughout her unspeakable ordeal, she said God's presence kept her alive.

Then suddenly one day, His presence seemed to leave her.

She writes that her prayers traveled no higher than the ceiling. Her words, "There seemed to be no sounding board."

When I have doubts, I turn to the Psalms. They help tame my emotional roller coaster.

But there is one Psalm that baffles me. It's the only one of 150 that doesn't end with hope and a renewed heart. **(Psalm 88)**.

The writer begins with a list of troubles—forgotten, overwhelmed, helpless and alone. God has "hidden His face."

The last word of the Psalm: "darkness."

He must have felt like Darlene. Both needing a comforting word from God. They got nothing. Maybe you relate.

Yet even in the midst of silence, they did three things:

- They came to God when they didn't "feel Him."
- They trusted the One who allowed their troubles.
- They persisted in prayer "day and night."

Their biggest tests are ours: Suffering, Aloneness, Silence. The last one is the hardest by far. The Silence of God.

During our lowest of lows, faith is simply taking God at His Word.

In the end, Darlene says, He spoke to me as I began to sing...

"When darkness veils His lovely face. I rest on His unchanging grace.

In every high and stormy gale. My anchor holds within the veil.

On Christ the solid Rock I stand. All other ground is sinking sand."

Selah.

# Our Cheerleader

When I read the Bible, I often try to guess how the writer will finish a sentence.

I did this recently: "When you show mercy do it with ****." ***(Romans 12:8)***

I put in "kindness" or "perseverance". I was wrong.

We are urged to show mercy with cheerfulness.

Cheerfulness? Yes.

There's a deadening idea among Christians that good works don't really count if you enjoy them.

As though enjoyment poisons the deed if it brings personal satisfaction.

Spiritual Hogwash.

A woman named Nano Nagle... yes, that name alone makes me cheerful... gave her life to sharing the gospel with poor children in the 1700's.

She wrote, "I often think my teaching will never bring me to heaven, because I only take delight and pleasure in it."

The audacity... to have fun doing the Lord's work!

Now, let me be very clear: her good works don't take anyone to heaven. It's only by faith thru grace in Jesus. **(Ephesians 2: 8-9)**

But the Bible takes us further. It says God "delights with pleasure" showing mercy. **(Micah 7:18)**.

At the Right Hand of God are pleasures forevermore **(Psalm 16:11)**. Guess Who's seated at His right Hand?

The Bible says God loves a cheerful giver **(II Corinthians 9)**. Jesus endured the Cross for the Joy set before Him.

God is holy and certainly expects our awe. People fall down in His presence.

But without sounding flippant, I also see Jesus as my biggest Cheerleader. He roots me on. Our advocate.

And oh, do we ever need it. God knows how hard it is to be us. **(Psalm 103:14)**

Be honest. Have you ever thought of Jesus being cheerful?

We are urged to be like Him.

Well, Cheers!

# Night Shift

I used to think sleeplessness was right next to Godliness. Not any more.

Now I often think the most spirtual thing you can do is get a good night's sleep.

Yes, I know the stories about missionaries who awoke at 2 a.m and prayed until 4 a.m.

Puritans who "renounced sleep" to redeem the time. Psalmists who prayed at midnight and woke before dawn.

Even our Savior who rose very early and went through the night without a wink.

The Proverbs do come down hard on the sluggard who hears his mother's call and mumbles "A little more sleep, a little slumber."

As a new Christian I thought there was no time to lose. Sleep seemed like an 8 hour paralysis on my way to winning the world.

An irritating interruption.

Then I read about a character named Elijah who was so depressed in ministry he wanted to die. God's remedy?
Sleep. Then eat. Then sleep some more. Some very practical theology.

The Bible says, "He gives to His beloved even in his sleep." And "He who keeps you will not slumber."

God works the night shift.

The One who knit my body stands beside my bed and reties my loose ends, patches and repairs me. Sleep is a healer.

When do you think I'm most vulnerable to impatience, irritability, cynicism and grumbling?

It's when my mind cannot turn off. Or I take on stuff I was never intended to carry.

One of my favorite scenes in the Bible is when the Sea of Galilee rages, the disciples freak out, and Jesus is asleep in the boat.

Have you ever noticed that God works His greatest wonders during deep sleep? In Eden it was Adam who slept as Eve is formed.

Abram sleeps as God gives a staggering promise of unconditional love. *(Genesis 15)*

And in Gethsemane, the disciples sleep as Jesus wrestles for our salvation.

Sure, the Bible comes down very hard on laziness. Sluggardliness is condemned. We're not talking about sloth.

Sleep is one of God's greatest gifts. It reminds us we are not in charge.

Here's a simple thought that helps me: Just because I go to sleep doesn't mean the Lord does.

So as childlike as this sounds… just give it to Jesus.

And go to bed.

Made in the USA
Coppell, TX
10 February 2024

28865631R00079